African American Criminologists, 1970–1996

African American Criminologists, 1970–1996

An Annotated Bibliography

LEE E. ROSS

Bibliographies and Indexes in Afro-American and African Studies,
Number 36

Greenwood Press
Westport, Connecticut • London

Library of Congress Cataloging-in-Publication Data

Ross, Lee E., 1958–
    African American criminologists, 1970–1996 : an annotated
bibliography / Lee E. Ross.
        p.   cm.—(Bibliographies and indexes in Afro-American and
African studies, ISSN 0742–6925 ; no. 36)
    Includes bibliographical references and index.
    ISBN 0–313–30150–6 (alk. paper)
    1. Criminal justice, Administration of—United States—
Bibliography.   2. Criminal law—United States—Bibliography.
3. Afro-Americans—Bibliography.   I. Title.   II. Series.
Z5703.R668   1998
[HV9950]
016.364′973—DC21   97–52329

British Library Cataloguing in Publication Data is available.

Library of Congress Catalog Card Number: 97–52329
ISBN: 0–313–30150–6
ISSN: 0742–6925

First published in 1998

Greenwood Press, 88 Post Road West, Westport, CT 06881
An imprint of Greenwood Publishing Group, Inc.

Printed in the United States of America

The paper used in this book complies with the
Permanent Paper Standard issued by the National
Information Standards Organization (Z39.48–1984).

10 9 8 7 6 5 4 3 2 1

For Leslie Ann, Christopher, and Alexander:
Those who make life worthwhile

Contents

Preface

Over the last ten years, criminal justice programs nationwide have witnessed a respectable increase in the relative numbers of African American criminologists and practitioners into the discipline. Our increased presence has prompted (if not mandated) a rethinking of traditional "mainstream" responses to issues of crime and justice. Whether it is the cause of crime within the African American community or the potential benefits of an Afrocentric perspective for offender rehabilitation, African American criminologists have advanced some excellent ideas. Despite our best efforts, however, these contributions are overlooked and rarely incorporated into criminal justice curricula, policy, and decision-making processes. Given the overrepresentation of fellow African Americans "entangled" in the encompassing mesh of America's criminal justice systems, it is *unusually ironic* that our contributions have remained relatively obscure. Because of this fact, the importance of recognizing our contributions and their potential to improve the "system" cannot be overstated. Perhaps our contributions are neglected because other scholars and practitioners are not certain of where to access our work, or for that matter, whom to look for? (In fact, some have even asked: What exactly is an African American criminologist?)

When confronted with the former question over sixteen years ago while still a graduate student at Rutgers, I knew of but two existing sources at that time. One source was Dr. Helen Taylor Greene's (1979) seminal publication: *A comprehensive bibliography of criminology and criminal justice literature by black authors from 1895 to 1978.* Another invaluable source was the *Index to minorities & the criminal justice system* (SUNY Albany, 1981). Those fortunate enough to have secured these books were quickly exposed to works that were comprehensive, interdisciplinary, and historical. To this date, however, efforts to document the scholarly contributions of African American criminologists (exclusively) are nonexistent. Therefore, in contrast to the pioneering works cited above, the first edition of this reference book is devoted *exclusively* to scholarly contributions of African American criminologists. In the process, it exposes readers to the names of many white and minority colleagues whom we have collaborated with while conducting research.

Admittedly, such an exclusive focus carries a heavy price tag. For example, we lose the ability to instantly reference the works of notable scholars from other disciplines who have greatly influenced African American thought on issues of crime and justice. Noticeably absent are the contributions of historical figures, such as W.E.B. Du Bois, whose *Philadelphia Negro* (among others) ranks among the first studies to examine the relationship between [African Americans] and crime. Equally worthy of inclusion, but absent here, are the inspiring contributions of Archibald Grimke, Ira De A. Reid, E. Franklin Frazier, Frantz Fanon, and other literary giants of previous eras. Likewise, we fail to include African American scholars from other disciplines, such as psychology, sociology, and economics (though many of us have Ph.D.'s in sociology and other disciplines). Their contributions to the study of crime and justice are equally worthy of acknowledgement. To keep this project manageable, my primary goal was to provide a handy reference guide to the scholarly publications of (contemporary) African American criminologists (who work in higher education). My rationale is that it is better to start with ourselves, rather than with others (especially when providing answers to the proverbial question: What have *we* done to make things better?).

WHO IS INCLUDED?

All contributing authors were initially identified from those listed in the *African American Criminology and Criminal Justice Directory* (Heard and Bing, 1995). Scholars found in this directory were cross-referenced to scholars in the membership directories of the American Society of Criminology (ACS), the Academy of Criminal Justice Sciences (ACJS), and the National Organization of Black Law Enforcement Executives (NOBLE). As expected, there was tremendous overlap among the three directories. Other potential contributors were identified through snowball sampling, personal contacts, and word of mouth. Once identified, potential contributors were personally invited to submit three abstracts of their publications. Invitations were also posted over the Internet (via the listserv for "Black Criminologists"). Therefore, those included in this reference book are those who (basically) responded to the invitation. As for those who failed to respond, my research staff "beat the bushes" trying to locate at least one entry from them. All totaled, 80 percent of the African American criminologists identified by Bing and Heard (1995)--excluding graduate students and non-academic practitioners--are included in this reference book. It is important to note that some of the publications resulted from collaborative efforts of white scholars as well. Such publications were included if at least one of the contributing authors was African American (**boldfaced** throughout).

Most of the contributing authors submitted the three abstracts requested. Some submitted more than three (given their publication records), and some submitted whatever few they had (reflecting, in part, their recent arrival into academia). Given the wide range in the number of abstracts submitted, I thought it both wise and fair to limit each author to four entries (except in a few instances). Often, the authors wrote their own abstracts (which explains, in part, the varying lengths of the abstracts included here). In other instances, existing abstracts were either edited or included in their present form.

These abstracts are by no means exhaustive, nor do they reflect the full range of our research interests. Because of space limitations, I had to be selective, even among our most published scholars. For example, three contributors in particular (John Austin, Coramae Mann, and Phillip Secret) had enough combined publications to fill this entire book. Others, such as Katheryn Russell, William Oliver, Leon Pettiway, and Frankie Bailey have written books since this manuscript went to press. Therefore, the abstracts listed here do not capture the full spectrum of our publication efforts. These abstracts merely reflect my attempted use of discretion and fairness. Most of the abstracts refer users to publications within mainstream criminal justice journals and periodicals. In addition to these, are selected books, manuscripts, and an array of state and government documents that provide, for the most part, Afrocentric perspectives on issues of crime and justice. It is important to keep in mind that while we are all "African Americans," all of us have not adopted, or espoused, an "Afrocentric" perspective (per se).

A quick glance through this reference book, though, reveals a cadre of African American criminologists whose research interests and responses to crime arguably differ from those of mainstream white criminologists. A common sentiment echoed in some of the works is that many of our contributions have been devalued and neglected by the mainstream of criminology, sociology, and related disciplines (see Young and Sulton, 1991, among others). Therefore, in presenting this edited reference book, my purposes were twofold: (1) to give users a handy reference guide to the scholarly contributions of African American criminologists, and (2) to showcase some excellent work as well as our research interests. In the process, it is my sincere wish that these contributions encourage our colleagues, practitioners, and policy makers to become aware of, consider seriously, and incorporate our contributions into their criminal justice decision-making processes.

This reference book consists of five sections: (1) an introductory article on issues that define (and confront) African American criminologists, (2) published abstracts, listed alphabetically by contributing authors, (3) selected references to each publication, (4) an appendix containing titles of doctoral dissertations for all contributing African American scholars, and (5) an author and subject index. In instances where authors (and colleagues) are cited in the abstract, readers are referred to the original publication for the full citation.

The following article, "Dual Realities and Structural Challenges to African American Criminologists," is included to inform readers of some issues that affect African American criminologists in our discipline. It is reprinted here with special permission from the Academy of Criminal Justice Sciences (ACJS). The article was written while I served as Program Chair for the 1996 ACJS Las Vegas meetings. The national response to this article was overwhelmingly positive and occasionally negative (by some who may have felt threatened by its message). Either way, my coauthor, Dr. Harvey L. McMurray, and I thought we would share it with you. When read with an open mind, answers to the earlier question, "What exactly is an African American criminologist?" become painfully clear.

Acknowledgements

I am deeply indebted to many individuals for their assistance and guidance with this book. A heartfelt thanks to Nita Romer, of Greenwood Publishing Group, for recognizing the importance and potential appeal of this book. Her patience and understanding set the tone for a good working relationship. I am equally greatful to Jane Lerner, production editor, for her remarkable insights, suggestions, and attention to detail.

The Research Support Office of the School of Social Welfare at UW-Milwaukee was especially kind in awarding a small grant to fund this research. Their financial support made it possible to revisit the Schomburg Center for Black Culture in New York. With its impressive collection of historical documents, it is, in deed, an invaluable resource.

Special thanks to Jeff Gold of the School of Library and Information Science who was instrumental in gathering data for this project.

I would also like to thank all of the African American criminologists for submitting copies of their publications. Without their cooperation, this would be yet another dream deferred. Special thanks to my colleagues Willie Edwards and Darnell Hawkins, whose wisdom, words, and deeds provide a constant source of inspiration.

Lastly, a posthumous thanks to the lady in my life, Geneva T. Ross, whose motto was: *"once a job has begun, do not stop until it is done--whether the labor is big or small, do it well or not at all."* Toward that end, I hope this work is pleasing in her sight.

"Dual Realities and Structural Challenges of African American Criminologists"

This article reflects significant issues and challenges based on discussions among African American criminologists over the years. Moreover, it reflects the thoughts of two African American criminologists, and is not intended to speak for each of our African American counterparts. Nor, for that matter, is the article intended to be a blanket indictment of our white colleagues. We challenge each of our white colleagues to remain objective and not dismiss or minimize our perspectives as irrelevant because they do not see themselves as part of the problem, or even worse, do not realize that a problem exists. Furthermore, we challenge our African American colleagues to promote and support sustained efforts to heighten African-American participation in research, scholarship and social as well as public policy reforms.

Throughout this article we attempt to provide a candid and realistic account about painful and troublesome issues, and thank the Academy of Criminal Justice Sciences for this opportunity. We should all view this article as an opportunity to dialogue about issues of concern to our national interest. Originally, we conceived this article as synonymous with "pet peeves" of African American criminologists. However, after several animated discussions we quickly realized that the issues, such as Afrocentricity, ethnic valuation, the media, campus environments, and community outreach, are much more than that. These issues share a dual reality. We could say that they are silent, yet highly vocal. They are nonexistent, yet widespread. Often they irritate our conscience and sometimes they trouble our souls. Never, do they disappear.

We have found that a common issue and challenge throughout much of our discussions in writing this article is *racism*, intended or unintended. Moreover, we regard racism as the vital and most challenging critical issue facing our great Nation. Our dual realities (i.e., differences in life experiences) become more apparent with debates surrounding Affirmative Action and events such as the Million Man March and the O.J. Simpson trial. A white male, who is also a dear friend, asked after the March, "What are *Black* men going to do after the March?" While an interesting question, it was the wrong question. More appropriately, "How are we as individuals, of all ethnic groups, going to evaluate and activate our individual efforts in the promotion of race relations and justice?" Our mutual resolve will reflect our collective legacy to promote a better quality of life and justice for all.

THEORETICAL NORMS VS. AFROCENTRIC PERSPECTIVES

Beyond the obvious void between theory and policy, the enterprise of theory development is largely centered around Eurocentric and Androcentric values. Hence, both the object and content of criminological theory have concentrated on criminal behavior of the more vulnerable populations, and for the most parts are culturally biased. This is not to suggest that such perspectives are without merit. Rather, they tend to be ahistorical and indifferent to racism and experiences of disenfranchised populations. African American criminologists can help overcome the aforementioned pitfalls. Turner (1992, p. 36) notes, "The Afrocentric perspective implicitly contends differences in culture, world view, and [that] historical perspectives exist between African Americans and Europeans, as are there differences between Asians and Europeans, many of which have implications for the construction of paradigms of human behavior." To paraphrase

Young and Sulton (1991), African American perspectives are virtually excluded from major treatises on criminology and criminal justice. [They] have been excluded primarily because we challenge many of the basic assumptions proposed by white scholars.

Inherent in most criminological theories is the presumption of individual pathologies, rather than structural factors prompted by racism and economic disparities. To paraphrase Dr. Charles King we have a society that has crippled a people--then blames them for limping. The same is true of criminality, which argues for a multicultural-based approach to criminological theory. Failing to incorporate a multicultural-based approach will continue to foster a peculiar arrogance among white criminologists and their student proteges, and alienation among their African American counterparts.

There is also the issue of research agendas of funding agencies that tend to favor Eurocentric research priorities that in turn impact theoretical orientations. While African Americans are often targets of research and disproportionately affected by social policy, African American criminologists are infrequently involved in outlining research priorities of policy and program development. For example, during 1994 an estimated 6.8 percent of all African American male adults were in jail or prison compared to less than one percent of white male adults (Johnson, 1995). The fate of African American males is of particular concern to many of us, yet we find ourselves outside the "loop" of decision-making and in providing solutions. To remedy this, we recommend that our white colleagues do more to include African American criminologists where opportunities exist, such as collaborating on research projects, publishing opportunities, involvement in grants, serving on editorial boards, and participating in policy-making decisions.

DISENFRANCHISEMENT VS. VALUATION

The term *disadvantage* implies that select social outcomes are, for the most part, linked with individual initiative. No, we are not bleeding heart liberals; we very much support the need for individual responsibility. We prefer the term disenfranchisement, however, because of the emphasis placed on the systemic exclusion and the concomitant need to address structural barriers rather than individual status. To what extent are African American criminologists involved in the advancement of criminological theory? African Americans can no longer passively wait for approval or acceptance of white criminologists to become proactive in theory building and asserting our place at the "For Scholars Only" table. The issue is directly linked to valuation and consistent with the old, but widely held adage that "white is right."

We understand that there are certain "rigors" to overcome in doctoral programs regardless of one's race. The experience is however different for African Americans in criminological/criminal justice doctoral programs---all housed in predominantly white institutions. Heard and Bing (1993) found that six out of ten African American faculty believe that their college professors were insensitive to issues of concern to them, and that approximately half believe they were victims of racism or discrimination by white professors. African American students often feel devalued by faculty and their white counterparts alike. A common retort often heard is, "How can that be; we have always been sensitive to these issues." Steele's (1992) article entitled, "Race and the Schooling of Black Americans" notes the process by which African Americans are devalued which results in a lowering of self-esteem, and culminates with a state of psychic alienation. "This psychic alienation--the acts of not caring--make him less vulnerable to the specter of devaluation" (p.74). Perhaps each of us should take a self-test and ask ourselves: To what extent do we encourage, in a real sense, expressions of diverse thought; what is our level of personal interactions beyond school; how has stereotyping influenced our perceptions of each other, and on and on?

An African American female doctoral candidate at a predominantly white university was asked to *retake* a graduate level theory course she had taken while attending an Historically

Black College (hereinafter referred to as HBCU). Again: Are white institutions presumed to be inherently better than HBCUs? These overtly (and often subtle) acts of racism touch the core of the issue of systemic devaluation that permeates our society. Moreover, Steele (p. 72) asserts: "Terms like 'prejudice' and 'racism' miss the full scope of racial devaluation in our society, implying as they do that racial devaluation comes primarily from the strongly prejudiced, not from 'good people' . . . ." To help eliminate these unsavory practices, Criminal Justice Departments nationwide should aggressively pursue opportunities to sponsor lectures and other colloquia that bring African American and white scholars to each other's campuses. In addition, the inclusion of African American writings and perspectives in the curriculum should be encouraged.

MEDIA TYPECASTING VS. INCLUSION

Three years ago, one of our African American colleagues, fresh out of graduate school, telephoned to discuss a new course she wanted to develop on *race and crime*. During our discussions, she requested that I send her a copy of my syllabus on race and crime. I wanted to help her--but I could not. I had never taught a course on race and crime. Yet, because I am African American, she assumed that I had. Much too often, our colleagues nationwide make similar assumptions (i.e., that we are better suited to discuss issues of race and crime, more so than other issues). We find these assumptions to be stereotypical. The media also typecasts certain scholars in our field. Whether it is the criminal trial of Rodney King, Susan Smith, or O.J. Simpson, the media seeks criminal justice experts to provide insights into these issues. When the issues involve race, the media seek an African American voice. In other issues, where race is not as evident, African Americans are generally excluded.

Perhaps the reason African American criminologists are not called on as frequently is because of the relatively small number of African American Ph.D. holders. At times, however, African American criminologists fear it is something more sinister. What if the media perceives white criminologists as more credible (not to mention more competent) than African American criminologists . . . . Sometimes, this reminds us of the annual Oscar nominations where Hollywood directors repeatedly cast whites in leading roles. Are we really surprised if Americans consider whites better actors and actresses? Something occurs very similarly to this in the field of criminal justice.

While our expertise varies considerably, some African American criminologists take exception to some white explanations and depictions of crime among African Americans. Many of us admire and hold in high esteem notable white scholars because they are worthy representatives of our profession. We question, however, whether these same individuals are "better suited" or even "the most qualified" to explain *all* dynamics of crime and justice as they relate to African Americans. In the context of criminological theory, for instance, perhaps nothing is more disturbing to African American criminologists than to have persons who may not fully understand the African American experience attempt to explain our people's behaviors. For example, it is almost as silly as having African Americans explain the behaviors of West Indian Americans (and vice versa).

When the media, in its many forms, continually employ the expertise of white criminologists, whatever the issues, African American criminologists are literally forced to remain silent on issues of tremendous importance and consequence to us and our communities. As it stands, African American criminologists do not have a national voice on issues of crime and justice. Although some of us may enjoy national exposure through academic circles, our influence on policy decision-making is minimal at best.

There is a critical need to identify African American criminologists to address these issues. We are quite disgusted with televised town hall meetings (and talk shows) on crime and justice that do not feature African American criminologists. We have seen politicians, celebrities galore and even hard core rap artists literally dominate the airwaves on issues of crime and justice. Quickly! What's wrong with this picture? This representation of African American culture clearly serves to perpetuate negative stereotyping. In addressing this problem, contemporary issues should include perspectives about the media and crime.

WHITE CAMPUSES VS. HISTORICALLY BLACK COLLEGES AND UNIVERSITIES

Perhaps the biggest decisions we make concern the kind of academic setting in which we work. Some of us have opted to teach at Historically Black Colleges and Universities while others teach at predominantly white institutions. Each choice carries certain advantages and disadvantages. At times, the most distinguishing feature between HBCUs and white institutions is having colleagues with whom to bounce ideas off, to provide guidance and mentoring, and to help us with our professional growth and development. At white institutions, for instance, rarely will you find other African American criminologists in your department. Despite all the rhetoric about Affirmative Action, white institutions seem to adopt a policy that "one is enough." This is a most painful and unfortunate reality. Still, again, perhaps it reflects the low numbers of eligible African American criminologists with terminal degrees in criminal justice and related fields. Colleges and universities *should not*, however, recruit African American criminologists based on Affirmative Action policies. We have worked too hard and too long to have our accomplishments diminished. At the same time, however, we recognize that ability without opportunity is nothing.

Equally disturbing realities are found in classroom settings. For example, some of us find it difficult to address a predominantly white classroom on issues of racial disparities and injustices within the criminal justice system. Moreover, insisting that some criminals are victims of injustice is bound to turn some students off. Through time, we may be pressured into placating our audiences by tailoring the context of our discussion to their social approval. This type of pandering affects us in many ways. For instance, it is difficult to be candid on some issues when these same students evaluate you toward the end of the semester. Often, to protect yourself from unfavorable evaluations, you are careful with what you say and in how you say it. Academic freedom--it is not. Nearly everyone receives negative student evaluations during their academic careers. The problem for African American criminologists at white institutions, however, is that we are often left wondering whether a negative evaluation is somehow racially motivated.

Although African Americans at HBCUs enjoy larger support networks, similar issues confront us as well. For example, some of us constantly battle the impression that our academic programs are somehow inferior to those of larger research institutions. Moreover, since most HBCUs emphasize teaching more than research, faculty members may not enjoy the academic freedoms to pursue publishing opportunities. The faculty at HBCUs is expected to compete with their counterparts with far fewer resources. For example, a dean from a prominent white institution commented on the cutback in dollars to support operations, noting a reduction in travel funds. This was a reality check and somewhat humorous when considering that some of *our* travel budgets rarely exceed $600 (for a five member faculty)! Beyond this, we (at HBCUs) teach four courses per semester, conduct research, chair theses, participate in university and community service, and publish with little or no institutional support. For some of us, we are left with the impression that colleagues and students come to devalue our contributions to the discipline simply because our names may not appear in the literature as often.

CAREER DEVELOPMENT VS. COMMUNITY ORIENTATION

For African American criminologists on white campuses, in particular, the dilemma of career development versus community orientation is very real. At research institutions, the pressures to publish are, at times, overwhelming (for whites as well).

Consequently, there is little time for other endeavors, especially community involvement. Simply put, one cannot do everything at once. Something has to give. More times than not, African American criminologists are not afforded the luxury of becoming heavily involved in community activities, despite many invitations to do so. We can, however, if we choose. However, choosing to do so would probably jeopardize one's chances for tenure. Whether it is serving on a new task force on domestic violence or the community advisory board, time is limited for these endeavors. This is where some of us wonder if we are doing the right thing, especially when issues of youth violence and high homicide rates plague our communities. At the same time we are expected to fulfill our obligations as role models for our youngsters. This seems like a catch-22 situation. Moreover, there are few (if any) rewards for such endeavors, and we have to wonder whether it works toward the detriment of more worthy goals. Community involvement should receive much more consideration for both merit and tenure decisions.

CONCLUSION

In the final analysis, it appears that each of us is a passenger on the ship named "SELF-INTEREST." We tend to promote what we regard as our legitimate interest without realizing we are connected to a common destiny, i.e., when the ship starts to go under--those on the upper deck will have a slight reprieve although their fate is certain, given the passing of time. It is disconcerting to hear *any* of our colleagues (whether African American or white) suggest that their "real" reason for attending a conference on crime and justice is to get a *vacation*. When we hear this, it reminds us of some familiar refrains. You know-- "different day-same story" or "same product-different packaging." Take your pick. At times, it appears that far too many white criminologists really do not care about the problems of crime in America, in part, because they do not perceive it as their problem. For example, we have witnessed leading white criminologists describe in breathtaking detail the hard core realities of African

American involvement in crime. Shortly afterwards, we witness the same individuals appear indifferent to the seriousness of crime in America, simply because they may not care beyond the point of discussion. For them, and some of us, criminal justice is merely a profitable enterprise--not to mention a very good conversation piece. This "act" should remind us all of Tony Platt's (1993) satirical essay that exposed to the western world how criminal justice professionals (and conference goers) conduct business. Call it satire if you will, but his depictions are all too real; just as real as Ralph Ellison's *Invisible Man* (which was supposedly *fiction*).

In effect, *"when all is said and done, more is said than done"* as we flock back to our suburban comfort zones. Who is to blame for this travesty and these cavalier attitudes of indifference? Each of us, African American and white alike, has the opportunity and responsibility to propel social justice forward. More importantly we have the collective skills, wisdom, and resources to make a difference as researchers, educators, and policy makers to enrich the lives of each citizen. Each of us is challenged (and hopefully committed) to make the aforementioned a reality. After all, is not our calling one of service?

REFERENCES

Ellison, R. (1958). *Invisible Man*. New York: Random House.

Heard, C.A., and R.L. Bing. (1993). "African American faculty and students on predominantly white university campuses." *Journal of Criminal Justice Education*, 4(1):1-13.

Johnson, D. (1995). "The Nation's correctional population tops 5 million." *Bureau of Justice Statistics*, 1-8, (Washington, D.C.: National Institute of Justice).

Platt, A.M. (1993). "How to overcome fear and loathing on the academic conference trail: Practical tips for beginners." *Social Justice,* 20(3,4):179-86.

Steele. C.M. (1992). "Race and the schooling of black Americans." *The Atlantic Monthly,* 269(1):68-76.

Turner, R.J. (1992). "Affirming consciousness: The Afrocentric Perspective." In *Child Welfare: An Afrocentric Perspective.* Joyce E. Everett, Sandra S. Chipungu, and Bogart R. Leashore (Eds.). (Pp. 36-57). New Brunswick: Rutgers University Press.

Young, V., and A.T. Sulton. (1991). "Excluded: The current status of African American scholars in the field of criminology and criminal justice." *Journal of Research in Crime and Delinquency,* 28(1):101-16.

Ross, L. E. & McMurray, H. L. (1996). "Dual Realities and Structural Challenges of African American Criminologists." *ACJS Today,* XV, Issue 1 (May/June), 1-9. Reprinted by permission.

African American
Criminologists,
1970–1996

Published Abstracts

BIKO AGOZINO

Agozino, B. (1996). "Football and the civilizing process: Penal discourse and the ethic of collective responsibility in sports law." *International Journal of the Sociology of Law* 24(2):163-88.

The dominant concern of existing literature is the inadequacy of legal regulations of sporting activities. The major concern of sports sociologists in this regard is how to deepen the penetration of sports regulations by the criminal law. This apparent "law and order" approach to sports and law research wrongly assumes that the principles and ethics of the criminal law would remain intact when reified and applied to the jurisdiction of sports. Moreover, experts on sports jurisprudence fail to show to what extent the criminal law has been "sportsified," the extent to which the criminal jurisdiction can be understood as a reflection of the logic and principles of sports performance and penalties. The present paper focuses on the ethic of collective responsibility for individual conduct that is understandably the dominant ethic of sports jurisprudence. This focus raises a serious question about the generalisability [sic] of this ethic to modern criminal jurisprudence.

Agozino, B. (1995). "Radical criminology in African literature." *International Sociology Association* 10(3):315-29.

This paper examines the way criminological theory is reflected in the treatment of the crime problem by African creative writers. In doing so, the author tries to show how the writers' views of the total society inform their representation of the crime problem. A criminological reading of the plays, *The Trial of Dedan Kimathi* by wa Thiong'o and *Mugo* and *Oga Na Tief-Man* by Fatunde; and the novels, *Devil on the Cross* and *The Contract* by wa Thiong'o and Iyayi respectively, demonstrates that criminologists should take creative writing seriously and creative writers should take criminology seriously.

Agozino, B. (1977). *Black Women and the Criminal Justice System: Towards the Decolonisation of Victimization.* Avebury: Aldershot.

This book demonstrates that victimization is not punishment. It is guided by the assumption that the more central punishment is to any theory or practice of criminal justice, the greater the tendency for that theory or practice to conceal or truncate relatively autonomous issues that are routinely packaged with, and thereby colonized by, the conceptual and institutional empire of punishment. Towards the decolonisation of victimization, the history of the victimization of black women in the guise of punishment is sketched from the days of enslavement, through conquest and colonialism, to neo-colonialism as a useful background for understanding the victimization of black women and other marginalised categories specifically in the internal colonies of England, with analogous evidence from other locations brought in to throw more light on the situation in England. The concept of colonialism is employed in this book to underscore the close links between the law-and-order politics of today and the imperial traditions of the past and also to emphasize the colonization of relatively autonomous institutions and processes by the criminal justice system. The major implication of the present book is that since the problems that face black women in the criminal justice system can be seen to result from the articulation of unequal and oppressive class, race and gender relations, research, theory and struggles must be aware of all three rather than prioritizing, disarticulating, isolating or reducing one or two of these relations.

ROY L. AUSTIN

Austin, R. L. (1993) "Recent trends in official male and female crime rates: The convergence controversy." *Journal of Criminal Justice* 21(5):447-88.

There is widespread agreement with claims based on official arrest statistics that male and female crime rates have not converged in recent years. Therefore, Adler's (1975) contrary claim is rejected and so by implication are earlier proposals linking gender differences in crime rates and unusually high black female crime rates to social roles and social status. The present study evaluated earlier studies reporting little or no male-female convergence in arrest rates. Also, it used Uniform Crime Report statistics, as have the studies often cited as contradicting Adler, and trend analysis to show that for 1965-1975 and for 1975-1986 the evidence for both juveniles and adults supports Adler. Even national self-report data previously said to contradict the convergence hypothesis have shown substantial convergence upon reanalysis.

Austin, R. L. & Arthur, J. (1992). "Family disruption, violent victimization and protest masculinity." *International Review of Victimology* 2(2):103-25.

Americans show great concern over the likely harmful effects of father-absent families on children, especially when families are black. Little or no concern is shown over step-families although these are expected to be the predominant family form by the year 2000. Our study finds the emphasis on female-based black households to be misplaced when violent victimization is the harm of interest. Data for 1973, 1976, 1980 and 1984 from national samples of Americans indicate that persons reared in both father-absent and step-father families were more likely to be victims of violence (being punched or beaten) than persons reared by both natural parents. The relationship was stronger for step-father families. Also, the only significant interaction between race and family structure (family type, family composition) showed a stronger relationship between family structure and violent victimization among whites. In addition, adverse effects of family structure occurred when family disruption was due to divorce or separation but not due to death of the father. The emphasis in protest masculinity theory on involvement in violence as an expression of exaggerated masculinity is inconsistent with the finding of no relationship when the father is dead and the relatively strong relationship when a step-father is present.

Austin, R. L. (1992) "Race, female headship, and delinquency: A longitudinal analysis." *Justice Quarterly* 9(2):585-607

Two recent studies support the hypothesis of a positive association between the "broken family" and crime; one repeats an earlier finding that this relationship is stronger for blacks than for whites. The alarm over the upsurge in female family headship in the United States led to a test of the hypothesis with previously neglected longitudinal data. For the years 1971 to 1986, despite tremendous increases in female family headship among blacks, only one of eight index offenses (arrests) showed an increase among black juveniles. Among white juveniles, increases in three of eight index offenses or total index offenses for black or white juveniles. The findings may be explained in part by changing attitudes toward birth outside marriage, divorce, and women's competence to rear children by themselves. Also, proposed explanations of the broken family/crime association, such as ineffective supervision by single parents and weakened attachment to single parents, are rendered irrelevant by our findings.

Austin, R. L. & Stack, S. (1988). "Race, class, and opportunity: Changing realities and perceptions." *Sociological Quarterly,* 29 (3):357-69.

Michael Hout provided empirical validation of the part of William J. Wilson's controversial 1978 claim concerning the increased influence of class on social mobility but not of his claim that the influence of race became less important than that of class. Anomie/despair as an indication of Americans' perceptions of life chances in 1973, 1976, 1980 and 1984 is used in this article. The findings show no agreement between perception and reality (that Wilson described) on the declining influence of race and the increasing influence of class. In addition, Wilson's dominant theme of deteriorating conditions for lower-class blacks and continuing progress for upper-class blacks was contrary to the data on perception. Barriers to continued mobility faced by more successful blacks is given as a possible explanation of the discrepancy between black mobility and black perception of life chances.

Austin, R. L. (1982). "Women's liberation and increases in minor, major, and occupational offenses." *Criminology* 20(3 &4):407-30.

Previous studies have been unable to determine a satisfactory starting point for female emancipation in order to examine the proposition that this variable caused an increase in female criminality. This study uses arithmetic coordinate charts and polynomial regression to set 1967 and 1968 as years when changes in female emancipation, as measured by female labor force participation and divorce rates, should be followed by noticeable effects. The same procedures also show take-off points for percentage female contribution to various criminal offenses occurring in close proximity and subsequent to exceptional changes in female emancipation and to the 1966 founding of the National Organization for Women. Contrary to the dominant position in the literature, increases in female involvement for the serious offenses of auto-theft and robbery, which may be attributed to women's liberation, are greater than increases in larceny-theft and fraud/embezzlement, which may be attributed to the same cause.

Austin, R. L. (1981). "Liberation and female criminality in England and Wales." *British Journal of Criminology* 21(4):371-374.

The recognition by social scientists in the early 1970s that female criminality had received little attention produced a flood of publications on women and crime by the end of that decade. Adherents of the women's liberation movement are likely to acknowledge their contribution to the recent attention criminologists have given this topic. But the contention in some of the resulting studies (Adler, 1975; Deming, 1977) that this movement has caused an increase in female criminality is understandably regarded as detracting from the movement's accomplishments.

Austin, R. L. (1980). "Adolescent subcultures of violence." *The Sociological Quarterly* 21(Autumn):545-61.

Wolfgang and Ferracuti's *Subculture of Violence* thesis and Matza's theory of "drift" may be regarded as competing subcultural explanations of violence. Comments are offered on studies examining propositions derived from both subcultural theses, and another body of evidence is analyzed. Ball-Rokeach's recent reaction to Wolfgang and Ferracuti's thesis is contradicted by a reinterpretation of her data and by the new data; for as both theses contend, violence is more likely among adolescent members of deviant subcultures and among adolescents with machismo or adult values than among other adolescents. Contrary to both theories, adolescent violence may result more from amorality than from a contracultural morality (Wolfgang and Ferracuti) or neutralization of conventional beliefs (Matza). Still violence is more likely among boys holding unconventional beliefs than among other boys. Also, poor relationships with parents or teachers are more important than class in insulating against conventional values.

Austin, R. L. (1978). "Race, father-absence, and female delinquency." *Criminology* 15(4):487-504.

Discussions of the influence of father-absence on delinquency often show special concern for the relatively high rate of father-absence among black Americans. However, for the four delinquent offenses studied, father-absence had detrimental effects only on whites, especially girls. The only significant effect among black girls was favorable to the father-absent girls. Further, contrary to Datesman and Scarpitti (1975), parental control has similar effects on delinquency and on the relationship between father-absence and delinquency for blacks and whites. It appears that policies which reduce the stigma of father-absence for white girls are more likely to succeed in reducing delinquency due to father-absence than policies of economic improvement.

Austin, R. L. (1977). "Differential treatment in an institution: Reexamining the Preston Study." *Journal of Research in Crime and Delinquency* (July):177-194.

Jesness' analysis of the Preston data offers no support for the utilization of Interpersonal Maturity Level Theory (I-Level Theory) to reduce parole violation among delinquents. The data are reanalyzed here and show interaction effects between I-Level and treatment for a specially selected psychiatric treatment unit. There are no interaction effects for other groups of subjects. The characteristics on which the psychiatric unit was selected do not appear to account for the results. Instead, there is evidence that treatment strategies were better developed in this unit. Findings on interaction effects in the psychiatric unit are favorable to the emphasis on differential treatment in California's Community Treatment Project and to some of the Project's treatment recommendations. Support for the use of the I-Level typology appears to have been limited by insufficient empirical testing of interaction effects, poor interpretation of findings, and conclusions drawn from inappropriate data.

FRANKIE BAILEY

Bailey, F. (1996). "The tangle of pathology and the lower class African American family: Historical and social science perspectives." In *Justice with Prejudice: Race and Criminal Justice in America.* Edited by M.J. Lynch and E.B. Patterson (pp. 49-71), New York: Harrow and Heston.

The paper examines African American family structure historically, and in the present era. It begins with a discussion of the Moynihan report, and moves to a review of literature that provides a better understanding of African American family structure. The importance of this research can be seen in criminology, where theories that associate family structure and criminal behavior are common. Given this connection, inaccurate depictions of family structure in African American communities yield a mis-understanding of crime, as well as inappropriate policies concerning a reduction of crime. This chapter provides the background on African American families needed to reinterpret the association between African American family structure and crime. More importantly, the article concludes that they there may be differences between ethnic group family structures within black communities that account for criminal involvement. In sum, a better understanding of the relationship between family structure and crime could result from the employment of a variety of research methodologies, both qualitative and quantitative.

Bailey, F. (1993). "Getting Justice: Real Life Vigilantism and Vigilantism in Popular Films." *The Justice Professional.* 8(1):33-51.

After discussing the history of vigilantism in the United States, this article examines the images of vigilantes and vigilantism presented in popular films. Scheur's guide to movies and the descriptions of films on video boxes were analyzed to find a body of films deemed representative of the vigilante film-type. An instrument for content analysis was developed and the films were divided into genre categories: action-adventure, classic, and contemporary drama. The findings indicate that the vigilante message is especially powerful as a credo with characters depicted as disillusioned law officers. The study suggests that the impact of these films upon the viewing public merits further study.

Bailey, F. (1991). "Law, justice and 'Americans': An historical overview." In *Justice with Prejudice: Race and Criminal Justice in America.* Edited by M.J. Lynch and E.B. Patterson. Pp. 10-21. New York: Harrow and Heston.

The investigation of racial or ethnic bias in the justice system is a complex task. Statistical analyses of current practices are often insufficient indicators of the presence or absence of racial or ethnic bias. Current practices which, on their face, do not appear to be outwardly biased, often hide practices, regulations, and laws that emerge directly from racial and ethnic bias. Thus, in order to evaluate the presence or absence of racial or ethnic biases, it is necessary to understand the historical origins of processes and attitudes that impinge upon current decision-making mechanisms. This chapter illustrates the importance of historical analysis to studies of racial and ethnic bias and demonstrates how the powerful employ law and justice against emergent minority groups.

Duffee, D. E. & **Bailey, F.** (1991). "A criminal justice contribution to a general education diversity requirement." *Journal of Criminal Justice Education* 2(1):141-157.

In the United States, colleges and universities have recently increased attention to diversity of faculty, staff, and student populations. Among the manifestations of the diversity movement are calls for modifications of general education courses to include coverage of cultural or human diversity. The authors review the objectives of the course, the teaching materials selected, and students' reactions to the first offering of the course. Among the most troubling reactions was students' resistance to history, to explorations of context of criminal justice practice, and to examination of current discriminatory policy and practice.

ROBERT L. BING III

Bing, R. L., Heard, C.A., & Gilbert, E. (1995). "The experiences of African Americans and whites in criminal justice education: Do race and gender differences exist?" *Journal of Criminal Justice Education* 4(1):123-41.

This study analyzes survey data to explore differences in experiences between African Americans and whites in criminology/criminal justice education. The experiences of females in criminal justice education are also explored. Written comments from the respondents on issues specific to gender and race discrimination are included. Findings point toward different academic experiences for minorities and females than for white males and to different experiences for minorities than for whites. Results suggest a need to address gender and racial biases as separate and distinct phenomena occurring in criminal justice academia.

Taylor, D.L. & **Bing, R. L.** (1995). "Racial discrimination in the juvenile justice system: Some unanswered questions." *Challenge* 6(2):5-28.

This article reviews the empirical literature on the role of race in the processing of juvenile offenders at every stage of the juvenile justice system. In general and specific comments, it points to the contradictions between research findings and policies, discusses the failure to implement the *Gault* decision, and stresses the need to consider the entire system as a process. In addition, it urges the use of a multistage research approach in future studies of various aspects of this issue.

Bing, R. L., & Harvey-Holmes, P. (1993). "Does race make a difference in the reporting of crime? A research note." *Journal of Research on Minority Affairs* 4(1):11-15.

This research note examines the reporting of violent crimes by the *St. Louis Post-Dispatch*, a major newspaper in a Midwestern city. The link between race, photographs, and the type of coverage is explored. Results suggest that less than 3 percent of the newspaper articles mentioned the race of victim or suspect. In addition, a pattern of downplaying the severity of crimes committed in the African American community, in favor of more expanded coverage for crimes involving white victims, emerged as a pattern.

Bing, R. L. (1992). "Politicizing black-on-black crime: A critique of terminological preference." *Journal of Research on Minority Affairs* 3(1):33-41.

This article argues that the phrase *black-on-black crime* is being overutilized. The phrase perpetuates negative images of African Americans. Problems emanating from use of this phrase and the need for conceptual clarity are presented. The issues of terminological preference, ethnicity, and race are addressed along with a discussion of negative policy implications and recommendations for movement beyond race-oriented research on crime.

Bing, R. L. (1991). "Fines and fines administration: Can the private sector fill the void?" *Judicature* 75(1):5, 50.

In recent years, the subject of fines and fines administration has received increased attention among practitioners and scholars. Many suggest that fines (as a criminal sanction) remain a vastly underutilized alternative to imprisonment. This underutilization is related to judicial ambivalence and a reluctance among court administrators, clerks, and probation officers to enforce fines when they are imposed. In fact, some court personnel concerned about their image and "status" within the court hierarchy have been unwilling to collect fines. The author argues that privatization is one method to invigorate the use of fines as a criminal sanction. Before doing so, however, international useages, judicial attitudes, and ambivalence about fines should be examined.

LEE P. BROWN

Brown, L. (1977). "Bridges over troubled waters: A perspective on policing in the black community." In *Black Perspectives on*

Crime and the Criminal Justice System. Edited by R.L. Woodson. Pp. 79-106, Boston: Hall.

As one of seven black criminologists convened by the National Urban League to address crime in the black community, the author highlights some of the racial injustices and social inequities that impact his job as a police chief. His address examines the police system by relating the police as an occupational subculture in the context of certain structural and organizational defects within police agencies. The pervasive problems of police in the black community viewed in the context of police discretion expose readers to a rare glimpse of the reality of policing. In concluding, the author suggests that the solution to the problem is one of decentralization and some form of police accountability, as opposed to gadgets and gimmicks that have been perpetrated upon the black people through police-community relations programs.

Brown, L. (1975) "New directions in law enforcement." In *Crime and its impact on the black community.* " Edited by L.E. Gary and L.P. Brown. Pp. 143-54. Washington, DC: Howard University Institute for Urban Affairs and Research.

The author presents the view that the present system for controlling crime has failed and that only through increased community support and involvement can we expect to make a meaningful impact on increasing crime. Adhering to the age-old adage that "an ounce of prevention is worth a pound of cure," the author advocates various potentially useful areas of research that include: (1) college education as a requirement for hiring police personnel, (2) police training, and (3) citizen complaint procedures, among others.

Brown, L. (1974). "The impact of crime and the criminal justice system on the community: An overview." In *Social research and the black community: Selected issues and priorities.* Edited by L.E. Gary. Pp. 88-98. Washington, DC: Howard University, Institute for Urban Affairs and Research.

The paper addresses the extent of crime within the black community. Furthermore, it encourages a rethinking of traditional approaches to crimes. White social scientists who [currently] dominate the field of criminology have not provided us with the answers we need, primarily because their approach has been *preventative* and reflective of a Western European concept of analysis. Therefore, black social scientists must begin to raise questions and challenge the stereotyped assumptions advanced by whites about crime among blacks and provide us with a new level of knowledge. The author concludes by outlining a research agenda for black social scientists. Included within this agenda is the effect of the fear of crime on the mental health of blacks, violence in the black community, crime and economics, and developing mechanisms to further promote black employment within the criminal justice system.

Brown, L. (1974). "The Police and Higher Education: The Challenge of the Times." *Criminology* 12(1):114-124.

As law enforcement agencies continue to increase their educational standards, it is incumbent upon colleges and universities to offer curricula that prepare policemen to meet the challenge of modern times. Criminal justice programs should pave the way for innovation and change in the police establishment by producing well-educated men, with a strong liberal arts background, capable of understanding self, community, and the role of the police in modern society.

SANDRA LEE BROWNING

Browning, S.L. & Cao, L. (1992). "The impact of race on criminal justice ideology." *Justice Quarterly* 9(4):685-701.

The existing literature contains conflicting theoretical positions and empirical evidence on whether race shapes perceptions of the criminal justice system. On the basis of a stratified community sample, the current study assessed these competing views. The data revealed that race was related significantly to criminal justice ideology; African Americans were found to be more and less conservative than whites. Racial difference persisted, moreover, when controls were introduced for general political ideology, crime experiences, contact with the criminal justice system, and neighborhood conditions.

CHARLES CORLEY

Nalla, M.K. & **Corley, C. J.** (1996). "Race and criminal justice: Employment of minorities in the criminal justice field." In *Justice with Prejudice: Race and Criminal Justice in America.* Edited by M.J. Lynch and E.B. Patterson. Pp. 139-55. New York: Harrow and Heston.

The relationship between minorities and the criminal justice system has been extensively researched. Much has been written about minorities' in the criminal justice system (especially the biases that confront minorities at each stage of the system). "An issue that has remained neglected, however, is the employment of minorities in the criminal justice system." This article explores: (1) the nature and extent of minority employment of personnel in law enforcement and corrections, (2) treatment of minority officers historically, (3) barriers to career enhancement and advancement, and (4) affirmative action programs and their impact on work relationships for minority employees. The implications of these findings are discussed.

Wordes, M., Bynum, T.S., & **Corley, C.J.** (1996). "Locking up youth: The impact of race on detention decisions." *Journal of Research in Crime and Delinquency* 31(2):149-65.

Prior research has produced inconsistent findings regarding the relationship between race and secure detention of juveniles. Many previous studies were conducted in single jurisdictions, had limited measures of offense seriousness, often did not examine the influence of social factors, and experienced sample selection problems. Using data on felony offenses in five counties, this study examined detention at three stages in the juvenile justice process: police detention, court intake detention, and preliminary hearing detention. Data were collected from case files in police agencies and juvenile courts to reflect actual offense behavior and the youth's family and social situations. Bivariate and logistic regression techniques were used to explore the issue of racial disparity. Findings indicated that African American and Latino youth were more likely to be detained at each decision point, even after controlling for the influence of offense seriousness and social factors.

Corley, C. J., Bynum, T.S., & Wordes, M. (1995). "Conceptions of family and juvenile court processes: A qualitative assessment." *The Justice System Journal* 18(2):157-172.

Prior research has not fully explained how the juvenile court uses family variables and how these variables influence decision making within the juvenile justice process. In this study, qualitative data obtained from interviews with court personnel across seven counties within a Midwestern state are used to assess how family factors influence juvenile justice processes and sanctions. Findings indicate that family variables influence judicial processing as well as sanction and placement decisions and that family variables as conceived by juvenile court personnel potentially place youth of color and poorer youths at greater risk for more intrusive court interventions. Moreover, results indicate that parental sponsorship is important for court officials in deciding how to handle youths. However, parental sponsorship, as Matza defined it, was framed within the context of parental control by juvenile court decision makers.

Payne, D.M. & Corley, C. J. (1994). "Police pursuits: Correlates of the failure to report." *American Journal of Police* 13(4):47-72.

Interest in police pursuits has permeated every branch of the criminal justice system and legislatures are considering limiting the practice of high speed pursuits. Arguments regarding the usefulness of pursuits are polemic. Some view all high speed pursuits as inherently dangerous, and opt for severe restriction or abolishment of pursuits. Others predict the dangers which could result if pursuits were abolished and take a position that the need to apprehend fleeing offenders outweighs the potential negative outcomes. Pursuit training must go beyond the traditional method and attempt to answer why things are the way they are. Officers must have a detailed understanding of the currently accepted meaning of negligence, foreseeability, emergency, the connections between environmental conditions and risk and the true purpose of pursuit policy.

Corley, C. J. & Woods, A.Y. (1991). "Socioeconomic, socio-demographic and attitudinal correlates of the tempo of divorce." *Journal of Divorce and Remarriage* 16(1/2):47-68.

This study assesses the impact of socioeconomic, socio-demographic, and attitudinal characteristics of husbands and wives on the timing of marital dissolution. The primary concerns were with divorce and the intervals of marital duration before divorce occurred. The analysis was based on an initial sample of 610 couples in the early years of marriage, all of whom resided within a large North Central Standard Metropolitan Statistical Area in 1978. The couples were re-interviewed seven years later in 1985 (N=544). The data collected from the first wave of subjects were used to identify antecedent characteristics of husbands and wives, whereas data from the second wave were used to measure the timing (tempo) of marital dissolution among the 105 couples who subsequently divorced. Partial correlation coefficients indicated that the tempo of divorce significantly varied according to the wife's employment status, occupational status, future work plans, father's education, age at marriage, gender role orientation and number of children. A multiple classification analysis of these variables showed that wives' employment status and number of children were the most powerful predictors of the tempo of divorce.

CHARISSE T. M. COSTON

Coston, C. T. & Finckenauer, J.O. (1993). "Fear of crime among vulnerable populations: Homeless women." *Journal of Social Distress and the Homeless* 2(1):1-21.

Previous studies concerning the fear of crime have identified certain vulnerability factors as being associated with higher levels of fear. These include, for instance, being female, living in certain ghetto areas, and being elderly. Because many of these studies focused upon fear in the general population, however, they assumed a certain homogeneity of fear, whether it be among women, among the elderly, among Blacks, etc. They failed to make distinctions based upon relative degrees of vulnerability. They also generally neglected the notion of fear management--of coping. This research focused on 200 homeless women who were living in New York City. Among other things, they were asked about their crime risks and their crime fears. Results indicate that fear of crime is higher among those street women who have suffered past victimization. It is also slightly higher among those who perceived themselves to be more vulnerable. Perhaps most interesting is the finding that there is only a low correlation between self-perceived vulnerability to victimization and the fear of crime. This supports the proposition that these are two distinctive concepts; and most importantly, it does so in the context of a particularly vulnerable population. Possible explanations of a seemingly paradoxical situation, namely high vulnerability existing side by side with a low fear of crime, are explored and discussed.

Coston, C. T. (1993). "Worries about crime: Rank ordering survival concerns among urban transient females." *Deviant Behavior: An Interdisciplinary Journal* 14:365-376.

This exploratory study examined the role that worries about crime occupies in the lives of New York City's homeless women. Building upon Coston's (1988) research finding of self-perceptions of high vulnerability but low levels of fear of crime among homeless females, the present study suggests that homeless women deprioritize worries about crime in lieu of worries about their family's well-being, poor physical health, lack of proper nutrition, and lack of money. Maslow's (1954) needs hierarchy is applied as an explanation of these findings.

Coston, C. T. (1992). "The influence of race in urban homeless females' fear of crime." *Justice Quarterly* 9(4):721-30.

This paper explores the differences between New York City's minority and non-minority homeless women in terms of the nature and extent of their victimization experiences while living on the streets, perceptions of vulnerability to victimization risk, and fear of crime. Results indicate that minority homeless women are victimized to a greater extent and are more fearful than non-minority homeless females. These results can be explained by differences in the routine lifestyles of minority versus non-minority homeless females while living on the streets.

Helal, A. A. and **Coston, C. T.** (1991). "Low crime rates in Bahrain: Islamic social control--testing the theory of Synnomie." In *Comparative Criminal Justice's Traditional and Non-Traditional Systems of Law and Control.* Charles Fields and Richter Moore (Eds.), New York: Waveland Press.

This pioneer work builds upon the systems of social control (synnomie) developed by Freda Adler (1983). Its intent is to assess the low crime profile of Bahrain and in so doing to offer explanations for this country's low crime rates. The unique situation in Bahrain is analyzed by providing an overview of the country and by examining recent crime statistics reported by official agencies in Bahrain and in the United States (especially in the state of Vermont). Although official sources of data do not provide reliable estimates of crime, Bahrain and Vermont are comparable in population size. This paper offers possible explanations of low crime by using as its base the theory of synnomie (i.e., the consistency of norm and values sharing). Conclusions speculate on the future direction of Bahrain and its ability to deal with crime.

Coston, C. T. (1989). "The original designer label: Prototypes of New York City's shopping-bag ladies." *Deviant Behavior* 10(2):157-172.

New York's vagrant population of females were interviewed in the main bag lady territory (between 30th and 52nd Streets), in Manhattan, in New York City. Ethnographic methods resulted in qualitative data about the forces that lead to lifestyles of living on the streets, day-to-day survival strategies for street existence and recommendations for policy intervention. A typology of shopping-bag ladies, while not found in the present study, is presented here for consideration and further development.

JULIUS DEBRO

Debro, J. & Conley, D. (1993). "School and Community Politics: Issues, Concerns, and Implications When Conducting Research in African American Communities." *NIDA Research Monograph, #30, U.S. Department of Health and Human Services.*

A discussion of politics of and barriers to conducting research in African American communities. Issues such as the kind of research that should be conducted, how to conduct that research and involvement of the community are central to this paper.

Debro, J. (1989). "Homicide in black communities: A public health perspective." *Ethnicity and Health* 7:179-201.

The study is looking at the movement of public health into the homicide arena. It focuses primarily upon a policy move by the Centers for Disease Control to redefine the correlates, causes, and consequences of homicide.

Debro, J., Murty, K.S., and Bonds, T. (1986). "Does income affect crime? An empirical analysis of black communities in Atlanta, Ga." *Journal of Southern Society of Economics* 13(1).

This is a study of the relationship between social class and crime. Two questions were asked in the study: Does income have an impact on the rate of crime and what are the significant predictors that are influencing criminal behavior. Four communities were involved in the study (two each from Atlanta, GA, and Washington, DC). "Analysis of data indicated that community infrastructure was much more important to crime than income."

Debro, J. (1977). "Institutional Racism within the Structure of American Prisons." In *Black Perspectives on Crime and the Criminal Justice System.* Edited by R.L. Woodson. (Pp. 143-60). Boston: Hall.

As one of seven Black criminologists convened by the National Urban League, the author examines the prison systems' shift in population from a majority of Whites to a majority of Blacks. Moreover, when the institutions were primarily White, the system was concerned with programs for rehabilitation such as work habits, schooling, counseling, and therapy. Now that institutions are primarily Black, the author notes a change in both strategy and terminology where words like imprisonment, fixed terms, and optional programs abound. The author refers to the new strategy as a form of institutional racism designed, in part, to insure that when the Black offender returns to the community, he is worse than when he was committed.

Debro, J. (1974). "Perspectives on blacks in the correctional process." In *Social Research and the Black Community: Selected Issues and Priorities.* Edited by L.E. Gary. (Pp. 105-111). Washington, DC: Howard University Press.

Prior studies indicate that the black offender is overly represented in the criminal justice system and valid reasons are given for this overrepresentation. Despite this, however, this article argues that incarcerated black offenders remain a neglected area of research. Regardless of where you start, research is needed not only on the state and federal levels, but within the military system of justice as well. The author concludes by encouraging blacks to dedicate themselves to the unselfish pursuit of helping others less fortunate than themselves. Furthermore, we should politicize our efforts by involving the Congressional Black Caucus, providing them with information concerning black criminologists and our research interests.

Debro, J. (1974). "The Black offender as victim." *Journal of Afro-American Issues.* 2:149-66.

This paper examines theories of black criminal behavior and attempts to answer the much broader question of whether discrimination exists within the criminal justice system at the federal level. It reviews various views towards explaining the disparities of punishment for blacks and whites in the criminal justice system. Two instruments were used to gather data from over two thousand offenders in San Francisco and Los Angeles. The data included demographic information, employment history, and criminal behavior. The study compared the experience of black offenders with white offenders. Results indicate that subtle and covert discrimination does exist in sentencing within the federal districts.

Debro, J. (1973). "Black lawyers in the bay area and the Black community." *Journal of Social and Behavioral Sciences,* Summer-Fall, 13-26.

This paper attempts to document and analyze the view that while black militant often express hostility to established white professionals, they are almost unanimous in selecting white lawyers to defend them on important cases with the police. An analysis of the reality of the black lawyers and their work patterns is analyzed. The narrative illustrates the many problems evident between black militants and black lawyers. While militants want competent lawyers, they are unwilling to provide the kinds of cases for black lawyers to develop a reputation for competence within the black community.

R. RITA DORSEY

Dorsey, R. R., & Giacopassi, D. J. (1987). "Demographics and work-related correlates of police officer cynicism." In *Police and Law Enforcement.* Edited by D. B. Kennedy and R. J. Homant. Pp. 173-88. New York: AMS Press, Inc.

Cynicism has been identified as an important theoretical construct that helps explain the police experience vis-à-vis the officer's perception of the world and, in particular, his perception of the work environment. This chapter will review the literature on police cynicism and add to the growing body of research on the topic by reporting the results of a study which specifies the relationship of cynicism to various individual- and job-related variables not examined by previous studies.

Dorsey, R. R. & Giacopassi, D. J. (1986). "Assessing gender differences in the levels of cynicism among police officers." *American Journal of Police* 5(1):91-112.

To determine differences in cynicism levels between male and female police officers, 89 female officers and 79 male police officers completed Niederhoffer's Cynicism Scale. No significant differences were found when comparing cynicism level and length of service of male and female patrol officers. Significant differences were found when testing the relationships of cynicism and rank and cynicism and education. It was concluded that although female officers adopt and manifest cynicism as do their male counterparts, significant differences are apparent in the assumption of cynicism between male and female officers.

OBI N. I. EBBIE

Ebbie, O. (1992). "Juvenile delinquency in Nigeria: The problem of application of western theories." *International Journal of Comparative and Applied Criminal Justice* 16(2):353-370.

There is no universal theory of delinquency. Cross-cultural studies of delinquency will help in identifying Western theories of delinquency that are culturally specific or culturally universal. This paper investigates the applicability of Western theories of delinquency to Nigerian conditions. The paper concludes the family-based theories [family attachment, poor parental characteristics, parent-child relationship, parental supervision, parental support, parental physical punishment (Glueck and Glueck, 1950, 1968; Nye, 1958; Gold, 1963; Reiss, 1975; Empey and Lubeck, 1971; Sutherland and Cressey, 1960, 1966; Hirschi, 1969; Jensen, 1972, and Grove and Crutchfield, 1982)], differential association (Sutherland, 1939), urban conditions (Shaw and McKay, 1942), economic conditions (Bonger, 1916), social control (Hirschi, 1969), and culture conflict (Sellin, 1938) are the most applicable Western theories of delinquency to Nigeria. Furthermore, theories such as poverty, broken-home, labeling, and gang membership are found to be inapt to explain delinquency in Nigeria. Additionally, obstacles to delinquency studies in Nigeria are delineated.

Ebbie, O. (1990). "Heads of state: The vice kings and narcotic barons." *International Journal of Comparative and Applied Criminal Justice* 14(2):112-124.

With historical records, this paper presents a descriptive analysis of the criminology of power. The paper traces the crimes of heads of state from the medieval to modern times. The various crimes of heads of state are delineated from Europe and Africa down to Asian countries. The author posits that the Machiavellian maxim that "the end justifies the means" is a false maxim as it destroyed so many human beings including the heads of state who pursued it. The paper concludes with noting the consequences of crimes of heads of state to society and particularly to the underprivileged elements of society.

Ebbie, O. (1988). "Juvenile justice system in southern Nigeria." *International Journal of Comparative and Applied Criminal Justice* 12(2):83-95.

This paper presents a descriptive analysis of southern Nigeria's juvenile justice system in order to show, through comparisons, what people of southern Nigeria consider to be juvenile delinquency and how they treat juvenile offenders. The method that more traditional societies such as those in Nigeria use in handling juvenile offenders may help in dealing with similar offenders in more advanced countries. Based on ethnographic observations in Nigeria and predicated on a review of ethnographic literature on Nigeria as well as a study of the Nigerian Criminal Code and Procedure, the paper suggests that the informal control of juvenile delinquency may be a panacea for recidivism and a consequent criminal career. It further asserts that governments should attempt to make the procedures and structure of the juvenile court, as well as the disposition of the juvenile, more informal than they are in most countries today by establishing neighborhood courts of lay judges.

Ebbie, O. (1985). "The correlates of female criminality in Nigeria." *International Journal of Comparative and Applied Criminal Justice* 9(1):84-95.

There is a great need to study female criminality in African societies. Therefore, this paper investigates the general characteristics of Nigerian female offenders incarcerated in a major woman's prison in Nigeria. In a preliminary study of female offenders in Nigeria, Oloruntimehin (1982) suggests that female criminality in Nigeria may be correlated with socioeconomic and family background variables. Consequently, the major task of this study is to find out the relationship between socioeconomic and family bond measures and female criminality in Nigeria. The offenses the inmates committed form the dependent variables. The data show that most of the inmates had a loose attachment to their families prior to the time they committed the offense that led to their imprisonment. Most of the offenders are lower-class persons. There is an inverse correlation between socioeconomic measures and involvement in property crimes (p = <.01). Also, there is no significant relationship between socioeconomic measures and crimes against persons. Family bond measures are significantly correlated with involvement in property crimes (p = <.001), crimes without victims (p =<.001), and personal crimes (p =<.001). But there is no significant relationship between family bond measures and involvement in smuggling contrabands. The inmates' criminality can be explained in terms of the breakdown of kinship ties and poor economic conditions in Nigeria.

Ebbie, O. (1989). "Crime and delinquency in metropolitan Lagos: A study of crime and delinquency area theory." *Social Forces* 67(3):751-765.

It has been postulated that "the crime and delinquency area" theory of Shaw and McKay (1942), which assumes that certain areas of the city are spawning grounds for crime and delinquency, is applicable to urban settlements in non-Western societies (Morris 1985). To investigate this postulate, ecological data are presented on the place of residence of criminals and juvenile delinquents and on the location of their offenses in metropolitan Lagos, Nigeria. These are discussed and contrasted with similar pioneer studies in the United States; then implications are drawn concerning crime and delinquency. But the research suggests that in the Lagos cultural setting the generator of heterogeneity is something besides physically deteriorated conditions. Indeed, heterogeneity in Lagos is characteristic of high and medium rent areas rather than low income areas.

WILLIE J. EDWARDS

Edwards, W. J. (1996). "Operating within the mainstream:

Coping and adjustment among a sample of homosexual youths."
Deviant Behavior: An Interdisciplinary Journal 17:229-251.

A sample (N=37) of African American adolescent homosexual males was administered a questionnaire that focused on four areas of social psychological functioning (self-identity, family relations, school-work relations, and social adjustment). The findings contradicted several past studies that reported in general that homosexual males experience crippling cognitive dissonance. Even with the existence of homophobia in the society, the adolescents were found to possess an adequate social psychological attitude and survival skills. The sampled adolescents reported being comfortable with their sexual orientation even though the majority of them had not disclosed their homosexuality. The respondents reported how they managed self-presentation among heterosexual persons. The adolescents appeared well-adjusted and stable in their social functioning and disagreed with the idea that they needed professional counseling.

Edwards, W. J. (1996). A measurement of delinquency differences between a delinquent and non-delinquent sample: What are the implications? *Adolescence* 31(124):973-89.

The present study compared 532 adolescents being detained by county juvenile authorities to 354 adolescents attending public school in reference to the volume of delinquent activity committed for a period of one year prior to the survey. Four levels of delinquent activity were developed, ranging from minor offenses such as runaway behavior to serious offenses such as assault. Participants were also compared on how they responded to several likert-type questions that measured factors associated with the inclination to commit delinquent acts (anomie, social bonding, delinquent peer association, labeling, and self-esteem). This comparison provided information on the multiple pathways to delinquency which suggested forms of intervention.

Edwards, W. J. (1992). "Predicting juvenile delinquency: A review of correlates and a confirmation by recent research based on an integrated theoretical model." *Justice Quarterly* 9(4):553-84.

A multi-theory model is used to develop an explanation for juvenile delinquency. Five popular theories (anomie, social control, differential association, labeling and self-esteem) are integrated into a causal model to measure the amount of variance explained. An R^2 of .29 was obtained. The integrated model was tested on 532 residents of a county juvenile detention center in a southwest city. The theories of differential association and anomie contributed the most to the model, while social control and self-esteem theories contributed the least. The moderate success of the integrated model of delinquent involvement suggests that more comprehensive delinquent measuring models should be tested by social scientists.

Edwards, W. J. (1992). "Constructing and testing a multiple-theory (integrated) model of juvenile delinquency." *Mid-American Review of Sociology* 17(1):31-43.

The present study positions constructs of five popular criminological/sociological theories into an integrated or multiple theory model to investigate the causation of delinquency. The model was tested on a sample (N=532) of males and females who were being detained in a county juvenile facility. The theories of differential association and anomie contributed the most to the model while social control and self-esteem theories contributed the least, leaving the labeling theory to contribute a moderate portion to the explanation of delinquency. The model indicated that the more anomic youths and those experiencing less social control were more likely to associate with delinquent peers resulting in higher labeling and lower self-esteem. A comprehensive model of delinquency is better structured to depict the sequential and progressive attraction toward delinquent involvement than single theory models.

LAURA T. FISHMAN

Fishman, L. (1994). "African American and Latino prisoners responses to a diagnosis of HIV/AIDS." In *African American Perspectives on Crime Causation, Criminal Justice Administration, and Crime Prevention.* Edited by Ann T. Sulton. (Pp. 149-76). Englewood, CO: Sulton Books.

This chapter examines the reactions of African American and Latino prisoners to a diagnosis of AIDS and the accommodative strategies these prisoners adopt in order to cope with the life threatening disease. The author identifies 60 African American and Latino male prisoners with HIV/AIDS incarcerated in five upstate New York correctional facilities. Data were analyzed with the "grounded theory" and constant comparative procedures." Previous researchers had found that common modes of accommodation included denial, passing, avoidance, and affirmation. Of the many findings reported, the prisoners' most common form of accommodation was to insulate themselves from anticipated rejection by others and at the same time to deny the presence of a life-threatening disease. An equally important finding was that a diagnosis of HIV infection did not necessarily deter intravenous drug users from behavior that can exacerbate the progression of the illness.

Fishman, L.T. (ed.). (1990). *Women at the wall: A study of prisoner's wives doing time on the outside.* Albany: State University of New York Press.

This book offers a comprehensive view of experiences of prisoners and their wives (N=33) both inside and outside of prison. Coping with the criminal justice system, stigmatization, negative family reactions, and feelings of shame, are daily reminders for these women whose lives have been affected by their husbands criminality, conviction, and subsequent incarceration. In the process, the author examines how the lifestyles of these women change before, during and after marriage to their convicted lovers.

It answers a host of complex questions, including, "Why do women get married and stay married to a prisoner," and "Is it safe to engage in conjugal sex with a spouse who may have a sexually transmitted disease?" Readers are introduced to terms like "neophytes," "old timers," and "fast livers," (among others). Interestingly, abuses of drugs and alcohol, economic and emotional dependencies, and spousal battering all characterize the relationships of some of the women and their prisoner husbands. Throughout this book, the author paints a fatalistic and frightening picture of the horrible socialization experiences of the men and the way some of these men treat their wives. Most interesting, however, are the many ways in which these women accommodate to their situations.

DANIEL GEORGES-ABEYIE

Georges-Abeyie, D. (1989). "Race, Ethnicity, and the Spatial Dynamic: Toward a Realistic Study of Black Crime, Crime Victimization, and Criminal Justice Processing of Blacks." *Social Justice,* 16(4):35-49.

This article argues against the thesis that the U.S. criminal justice system is "color blind." This thesis, as argued by Hindelang, Petersilia and Wilbanks, is explained and criticized on the basis that it lacks a social ecological perspective, focuses on the formal decision processing of Blacks instead of the informal decision making that is so important in understanding criminal justice decision making, and because this thesis inappropriately analysis Blacks as an ethnic monolith. An alternative view which rejects the Black ethnic monolith paradigm, highlights the spatial factor and its significance in criminal justice processing of Black defendants, and details the role of extralegal social controls in light of Black ethnic diversity. An explanation of the nature of systemic racism is offered in terms of "petit apartheid" practices evident in criminal justice agents and agencies practices that selectively demean the humanity of Blacks in the criminal justice system. This article concludes by offering the elements necessary for a realistic study of Black crime, the criminal victimization of Blacks, and the criminal justice system processing of Black suspects and defendants.

Georges-Abeyie, D. (1983). "The Social Ecology of Bomb Threats, Dallas, Texas." *Journal of Black Studies,* 13(3):305-20.

This article attempts to correct the absence of social science research on criminal bombing by offering a systematic analysis of bomb threats perpetrated within the spatial bounds of Dallas, Texas during 1975. Using U.S. Department of Justice data, the extent of such crimes in Dallas, Texas, are detailed and viewed in the context of bombings nationally. Social ecology and geography methods of analysis are detailed and employed to better understand bombings in Dallas. Findings indicate the motivation, type of bombing present, and characteristics of perpetrator. Suggests that a social ecology analysis could help explain or lead to the development of new theories of crime causation.

Georges-Abeyie, D. & Zandi, M. M. (1978). "The study of bombings, incendiaries, and bomb threats in the city of Dallas for the year 1975." *Journal of Environmental Systems* 8(1):57-97.

This study is concerned with the spatial as well as non-spatial analysis of bomb threats and explosions in the city of Dallas for the year 1975. Information in the form of bomb logs was provided by the Explosive Ordinance Unit, Tactical Services Section, Special Operations Division of the Dallas Police Department. The preliminary perusal of bomb log data for the calendar year 1975 revealed that 396 incidents concerning bomb threats and bombings were reported to the Dallas Police Department; however, only thirty-five incidents or 8.8 percent of the reported 396 incidents actually resulted in a bombing. Some of our most basic findings were the following: bombings which resulted in casualties or major property damage were rare; revenge was the most common motive; public buildings, business offices, and residential structures were the primary locations for incidents; the ethnic/racial characteristics of 43.6 percent of the suspects could not be determined; females tended to be underrepresented in the suspect category; bombings, incendiaries, and bomb threats were the actions of youthful offenders.

HELEN TAYLOR GREENE

Greene, H.T. (1994). "Black perspectives on police brutality." In *African American Perspectives on Crime Causation, Criminal Justice Administration, and Crime Prevention.* Edited by A.T. Sulton. Pp. 139-148. Englewood, CO: Sulton Books.

This paper was developed in an effort to identify black perspectives on police brutality. Emphasis was placed on identifying research, change agents and victims of police brutality. The identification process included reviewing literature in several special collections and libraries, including Howard University's Moorland Spingarn Research Center, the Library of Congress, Hampton University's Peabody Collection, and the libraries at Norfolk State University and Old Dominion University. A content analysis was completed of available research, significant historical and contemporary incidents of police brutality involving black victims, and black police officers' accounts. Information also was obtained from civil rights organizations and governmental agencies.

Greene, H. T. (1994) "Black female criminality." In *African American Perspectives on Crime Causation, Criminal Justice Administration, and Crime Prevention.* Edited by A.T. Sulton. Pp. 109-122. Englewood, CO: Sulton Books.

Throughout the 20th century the development of youth has been an important issue in the Black community. Studies of Black female delinquents, however, are rare. This is surprising, given the fact that as of 1990, Black women represented almost half of all female prisoners under state and federal jurisdiction. The author demonstrates that existing data sources are of limited use in determining the extent of delinquency, generally, and Black female delinquency in particular. Given the methodological problems of both official and unofficial delinquency sources, the simultaneous effects of race and gender are noticeably absent from the literature. In recognition of these limitations, the present study recommends a general research strategy for future research concerning Black female delinquency.

Greene, H. T. (ed.). (1979). *A comprehensive bibliography of criminology and criminal justice literature by black authors from 1895 to 1978.* Hyattsville, MD: Ummah Publications.

Since the turn of the century, Black social scientists have written extensively on the problems of crime and justice. Despite their contributions, however, these writings have been neglected by the mainstream of criminological and sociological literature. To partially address this concern, the editor compiled this bibliography to provide users with a research tool for identifying criminal justice and criminology literature by Black authors. This pioneering work is divided along four sections: (1) periodical literature, works appearing in edited volumes, and relevant chapters from books, (2) books, (3) special reports, and (4) theses and dissertations. In the editors view, the inevitable recognition of the writings of Black authors will contribute significantly to developing more effective crime fighting policies.

DARNELL F. HAWKINS

Hawkins, D. F. (1995). "Ethnicity, race, and crime: A review of selected studies." In *Ethnicity, Race, and Crime: Perspectives Across Time and Place.* D.F. Hawkins (ed.), (Pp. 11-45). Albany: State University of New York Press.

This chapter examines the refusal of contemporary social scientists (especially those examining the etiology of criminal behavior) to confront the question of the extent to which ethnic and social groups differ. In doing so, the author summarizes and critically reviews ten seminal works that have explored conceptual, theoretical, and empirical dimensions of relationships among ethnicity, race, and crime. Examined works include those of Du Bois (1899, 1904); Sellin (1928, 1938); Sutherland (1924, 1934); Shaw (1929); Shaw and McKay (1942); Bonger (1943); and Wolfgang and Cohen (1970). From these examinations, the author illustrates how the biases outlined by Pettigrew (1980) are manifested and how they contribute to both the strengths and limitations of these important works. Moreover, by presenting the specific historical context of each work, the author attempts to show that the themes and conclusions evidenced in the studies are consistent with DeGre's (1955) view of the social construction of social science.

Hawkins, D. F. (1993). "Inequality, culture, and interpersonal violence." *Interpersonal Violence* (Winter):80-94.

Policymakers often are at odds over what strategies will be most effective at reducing the incidence of violent behavior in high-risk populations. Beginning with the position that social theory and public policy are inextricably linked, the author examines the policy implications of the long-standing debate in the social sciences over the relative contributions of socioeconomic inequality versus cultural differences as causes of violence. While the weight of the scholarly evidence favors neither of these explanations, existing and proposed policies often reflect a preference for the importance of culture. This paper discusses the limitations of that choice and advocates alternative policies that consider the importance of both sets of etiologically factors.

Hawkins, D. F. (1990). "Explaining the black homicide rate." *Journal of Interpersonal Violence* 5(2):151-163.

Despite the disproportionately high rate of homicide among African Americans, social scientists have offered few theories to explain this phenomenon. However, the absence of explicit theory has not meant that researchers have failed to consider questions of the etiology of homicide among Blacks. Implicit theory derived from traditional, liberal race relations research has been an integral part of quantitative studies of Black homicide. This article reviews and critiques these explanations for racial difference in the rate of homicide and notes the extent to which they have been challenged by recent scholars.

Hawkins, D. F. (1987). "Beyond anomalies: Rethinking the conflict perspective on race and criminal punishment." *Social Forces* 65(3):719-745.

Research on race and punishment for crime has produced inconsistent findings. Most previous reviews of the literature have been focused primarily on the numerous methodological flaws that may give rise to such inconsistencies. In this paper the author suggests that inconsistent or anomalous findings in this area of research may also result from problems of conceptualization and theory. More specifically, it is argued that the conflict perspective must be substantially revised to begin to account for various anomalies observed by empirical researchers. Such a need for revision is the consequence of both problems in the original formulation of the perspective and its oversimplification within the empirical literature.

Hawkins, D. F. (1986). "Race, crime type and imprisonment." *Justice Quarterly* 3(3):251-269.

This paper largely replicates, within the state of North Carolina, Blumstein's (1982) national study of the effects of arrests on the racial disproportionality of the prison population. In agreement with the previous study, these data indicate that the racial difference between rates of arrest and imprisonment varies with the type of offense. The level of arrests failed to account for a sizable amount of the racial differentials in imprisonment for drug offenses, forgery and driving under the influence. An unexpected finding is a lower than expected (by arrests) rate of black imprisonment for rape and robbery.

CHINITA A. HEARD

Heard, C. A., Ludwig, W. G., & Bing, R. L. (1996). "Correlates of drug use among African American arrestees: The case for multi-cultural approaches." *The Journal of Research on Minority Affairs* 3:3-10.

Widespread concern about the magnitude and characteristics of illegal drug use, particularly crack cocaine, prompted local criminal justice officials to implement a drug testing program between June and October 1990. Data are utilized to determine the need for treatment-based strategies with and emphasis on multi-cultural services and sensitivity training. To accomplish this, we analyzed demographic characteristics of arrestees who tested positive for drugs while being held at Allen County Lockup in Fort Wayne, Indiana. Results show that African American arrestees are in greatest need of drug intervention strategies for crack cocaine use, while White arrestees are in greatest need of alcohol intervention.

Heard, C. A., & Bing, R. L. (eds.). (1995). *African American criminology and criminal justice directory.* Arlington: University of Texas at Arlington.

This directory provides a comprehensive guide to African American criminologists and criminal justice practitioners. The editors provide information along five categories, including (1) doctoral students in criminal justice/criminology programs, (2) African American criminal justice faculty members, (3) African American criminal justice administrators, (4) doctoral students by graduate program, and (5) faculty administrators by state. Representing an improvement on the first edition (1993), this directory contains an up-to-date listing of nearly all African American scholars and practioners of criminal justice. A unique feature of this directory is that it lists the areas of research interests of each scholar/practitioner in addition to their institutional and agency affiliation.

Heard, C. A. & Bing, R. L. (1993). "African American faculty and students on predominantly white university campuses." *Journal of Criminal Justice Education* 4(1):1-13.

This paper stresses improving institutional climates by properly addressing issues affecting African American students and faculty on predominantly white university campuses. We address concerns and experiences of the authors, and the shared experiences of other African American Ph.D. students in criminology and criminal justice, mentoring issues, and suggested responsibilities for university administrators. We include results of a questionnaire mailed to African Americans with Ph.D.s in criminology or criminal justice. The paper contributes to an awareness of difficulties encountered by African Americans on predominantly white university campuses.

Heard, C. A. (1993). "Forecasting models for managing a changing inmate population: Implications for public policy." *Criminal Justice Review* 18(1):1-11.

Among the most critical public policy issues confronting local, state, and federal officials is the rapid increase in the correctional population. By the end of 1989, a record-breaking 710,054 men and women were imprisoned. Unfortunately, overcrowded institutional conditions have caused an increase in inmate violence, inadequate staffing, and inadequate medical care, especially for the aging prison populations. Should these trends continue without appropriate intervention, the economic, social, and medical impacts of managing and operating correctional facilities may be devastating. A secondary analysis of a national data base was conducted in order to make population projections and to determine movement within age groups over time. Discussions of the application of a difference equation model and of subsequent implications for managing correctional facilities are also presented.

ZELMA W. HENRIQUES

Henriques, Z. W. (1996). "Imprisoned mothers and their children: Separation-reunion syndrome dual impact." *Women and Criminal Justice* 8(1):77-95.

Presently, there is concern regarding the imprisonment of female offenders who are mothers occasioned by both the numerical increase in women prisoners and by the fact that research and public policy have centered primarily on separation issues. It is estimated that 70-80% are mothers. Incarceration results in the separation of mothers and children. Following their incarceration, most mothers plan to be reunited with their children. This paper examines the reunion aspect and makes recommendations for its successful implementation.

Henriques, Z. W. (1995). "African American women: The oppressive intersection of gender, race and class." *Women and Criminal Justice* 7(1):67-80.

This article argues that African American women are not a homogeneous group. An attempt to categorize them will therefore establish that there are differences within the group as well as between African American women and other groups of women. African American women continue to be victims of racial oppression, sex discrimination and class stratification. Historical and contemporary forces which shape the lives of African American women will be identified.

Henriques, Z. W. (1981). "The human rights of incarcerated mothers and their children." *International Child Welfare Review* 49:18-27.

All children encounter experiences which have some degree of traumatic impact. Yet, children of incarcerated mothers have been so grossly and continuously exposed to traumatic events that their lives are misshapen in a sense. For some children these traumatic experiences begin prior to their mothers' arrest and subsequent incarceration. This article maintains that it is vital that the state consider the catastrophic repercussions its own decisions have on so many affected people.   To the extent that the state has the responsibility for exerting the weight of censure on the offender, it must devote equal effort to minimizing what its drastic sanctions do to those persons legally innocent, but tied to the offender by family or dependency bonds, most especially children.

JACQUELINE F. HUEY

Huey, J. & Lynch, M.   (1996). "The image of black women in criminology: Historical stereotypes as theoretical foundation."   In *Justice with Prejudice: Race and Criminal Justice in America.* Edited by M.J. Lynch and E.B. Patterson. Pp. 72-88. New York: Harrow and Heston.

This article examines historical stereotypes and prejudices about Black females found in popular culture and its effect on modern criminological theory.   Viewing Black women as disadvantaged and excluded from power as a consequence of their race and gender, the authors contend that the images criminologists draw upon are distorted. The distortions result from stereotypical images of Black women who have been viewed historically as either the "mammy," the "matriarch," the "welfare mom," or the "jezebel." Relying upon these images in the absence of a critically objective assessment leads to distorted images of Black women that appear in modern criminological theory. The authors stress the importance of using nontraditional, qualitative methods to expose biased treatment of Black women in criminological theory. Furthermore, Black women must challenge traditional criminology on the most fundamental levels of theory construction in order to transcend many of its gender and racially-based paradigms.

JEROME E. JACKSON

Jackson, J. E. & Ammen, S. (1996). "Race and correctional officers' punitive attitudes toward treatment programs for inmates." *Journal of Criminal Justice* 24(2):153-66.

The attitude of correctional officers is a crucial variable related to how the prison system acts, reacts, and interacts with inmates. The proposition that the induction of minorities into the correctional work place will induce more compassion toward inmate clients by reducing both tension and hostility within the prison is inconclusive. This paper examines the recent inclusion of minorities into the traditionally Caucasian male correctional officer's world within Texas prisons. Are minority attitudes toward treatment programs for inmates different from those of Caucasian officers? The observations and analysis of the data support the position that attitudinal variation among officers' attitudes are significantly related to the race of the officer. That is, the attitudes of minority officers toward treatment programs does appear to be statistically different from those exhibited by the traditional Caucasian male officer. Most interesting is the finding that the Black officers rather than the Caucasian officers are less punitive over time in their attitudes.

Jackson, J. E. (1996). "Fraud masters: Professional credit card criminals and crime." *Criminal Justice Review* 19(1):24-55.

In this country, credit card companies, banks, and retail establishments suffer losses totaling $2 billion annually as the result of credit card abuse and fraud. These enterprises suffered losses totaling more than $1.9 billion in 1990, 1991, and again in 1992. The credit and banking industries experienced no decreases in losses for fiscal year 1993, and the prognosis for reduction in losses during 1994 appears dismal. This study examines the working habits of a gang of credit card thieves, and covers a neglected area and criminal type. It describes and discusses a criminal system of a clique of professional thieves called fraud masters. These offenders are involved in credit card crimes. They are proficient in the art of securing these instruments of purchase and are willfully engaged in their abuse. Observations indicate that the criminal behavior of this gang of economic law-violators reaffirms the strength of theoretical formulations regarding professional crime and criminals offered by Edwin H. Sutherland (1937).

Jackson, J. E. (1996). "Computer crimes and criminals." *American Criminal Justice Association (LAE) Journal* 57(1/2):32-36.

This paper focuses on this relatively contemporary phenomenon in criminology and criminal justice--computer-generated economic crime. Theoretical perspectives and research efforts in this area are slowly beginning to emerge. Several authors have indicated the increasing need for law enforcement to improve its efforts at controlling the expansion of computer-generated offenses and computer criminals (Pfuhl, 1987; Sloan, 1984). In this article, the authors call for greater attention to this offense type and offenders.

Jackson, J. E., Wallace, P.H., & Wint, A.V. (1995). "The status of police officers' liability for negligence involving the use of firearms." *American Criminal Justice Association (LAE) Journal* 56:(Spring-Summer).

This paper examines the status of police liability for negligence involving the use of firearms. Several aspects of this issue are examined. First, it discusses case law in which the officer is liable for negligence involving the use of a firearm; second, it seeks to clarify the types of defense available to police officers involved in negligence in the use of firearms; and third, it analyzes the trends in officer liability.

Jackson, J. E. (1993). "Fraud masters: Studying an illusory, non-violent, gang specializing in credit card crimes." *The Gang Journal* 1(4):17-36, 1993.

Credit cards are important instruments of the American economy, with more than eighty percent of the population having a card with a checking account. Criminal abuse of these instruments is on the increase. Unlawful utilization continues at alarming and un-documented rates. Evidence of abuse is seen among individuals and groups that use these instruments as the basis of their livelihood. This paper describes and examines the procedures used to study a gang of unconvicted credit-card fraud artists. Acting in the capacity of investigative-observer and utilizing field research techniques, the author sought to explore the world of the fraud artists. The study of this select group of economic offenders, whom the author has intuitively named fraud masters, offers an opportunity to better describe and explain the behavior, attitudes and environments produced in particular social situations. A major result of the investigation was the realization that fraud masters and other non-violent gangsters, as unique and successful categories of economic offenders, can be observed and interviewed in their natural setting. In addition to documenting behavior patterns and identifying special environments, the investigator was also able to determine the process of co-opting and recruiting new members.

Jackson, J. E. (1992). "Deviance and change in the urban African American community." *Western Journal of Black Studies* 16(3):123-131.

This paper is an attempt to critically examine the present state of turmoil in disadvantaged communities. The presenter argues that the problems encountered today involving youthful offenders, violence, gangs, and crime, result from historic mistreatment and denial of those individuals and families dwelling in our festering slums, especially nonwhites. The writer then proceeds to call for the reversal of these impoverished conditions and hostile environments through peacemaking.

PATRICIA H. JENKINS

Welsh, W., Harris, P., & **Jenkins, P.** (1996). "Reducing

overrepresentation of minorities in juvenile justice: Development of community-based programs in Pennsylvania." *Crime and Delinquency* 42(1):76-98.

Although minority overrepresentation in juvenile justice settings has been identified as a persistent problem, interventions are scarce. To address overrepresentation in its juvenile justice system, Pennsylvania has funded nine community-based intervention programs. This article describes a systematic model that provides an active role for program staff in program assessment and development prior to the design of outcome evaluations. Using archival, interview, and observation methods, we conducted evaluability assessments and process evaluations of each program. These formative evaluations provided essential information to strengthen community-based program planning, implementation, and impact assessment.

Jenkins, P. (1995). "School delinquency and school commitment." *Sociology of Education* 68(3):221-239.

This article examines the influence of personal background characteristics, family involvement, and ability grouping on school commitment, which, in turn, affects the extent of students' participation in school crime, school misconduct, and school nonattendance. Survey data from a sample of 754 middle school students in grades 7 and 8 support the hypothesis that decreasing levels of school commitment are linked to increasing rates of school crime, misconduct, and nonattendance. Personal background, family involvement, and ability grouping help to explain the level of school commitment. Higher school commitment is associated with being female, white, in the eighth grade, and in high ability mathematics classes. Youths of more educated mothers and whose parents are highly involved in their schooling are also more educationally committed. School commitment mediates the effects of personal background, family involvement, and ability grouping on the school delinquency measures. These findings can serve as a basis for early school-based delinquency prevention efforts.

IDA M. JOHNSON

Johnson, I. M. (1995). "Family members' perceptions of and attitudes toward elder abuse." *Families in Society* 76(4):220-229.

The relationship between elders and their primary caregivers is examined by comparing their attitudes toward the definition, criminalization, and treatment of elder abuse. Interviews with a random sample of 50 elders in Tuscaloosa County, Alabama, were conducted, and a questionnaire was administered to their caregivers. Results suggest that the perceptions of the two groups are similar; both tended to define elder abuse in terms of neglect and to support its criminalization.

Curry, B. S., **Johnson, I. M.**, & Sigler, R. T. (1994). "Elder abuse: Justice problem, social problem, or research problem?" *Free Inquiry in Creative Sociology.* 22(1):65-71.

This study investigates the relationship between elders and their care providers. It focuses the definition and prevalence of elder abuse and advocates the criminalization of those who commit it. Results are based on interviews with 50 institutionalized elderly women from Tuscaloosa, Alabama. Based on both the characteristics and limitations of the sample, it was concluded that elder abuse may be better characterized as a social problem rather than a criminal justice one.

Johnson, I. M. (1992). "Economic, situational, and psychological correlates of the decision-making process of battered women." *Families in Society* 73(3):168-176.

Interviews were conducted with 426 battered women at a spouse-abuse shelter in central Florida in an effort to understand the correlates of their decision to return home to the abuser after leaving the shelter. Drawing upon the tenets of exchange theory, analysis suggest that these women are likely to return home for several reasons: if the annual family income is high, if they are unemployed, if they have been victims of severe abuse, and if they have negative perceptions of themselves. A battered woman's decision-making process varies with respect to her perceived level of rewards and costs.

DELORES JONES

Jones, D. & Brockett, R. (1995). "The role of the J.D. in criminal justice education." In *Issues in Criminal Justice: Shaping Tomorrow's Future*, N. Ali-Jackson (ed.), (Pp. 14-28). New York. McGraw-Hill.

A review of recent position announcements for vacancies in criminal justice/criminology departments reveals an increasing number of announcements that exclude those possessing the terminal degree of Juris Doctor from consideration for full-time faculty positions. This is so even though many of the departments offer numerous Criminal Law related courses and have tenured faculty with the same degree. This paper argues that this policy of exclusion is inappropriate for at least three reasons: (1) there is no evidence that others are more qualified to teach the law related courses; (2) it greatly reduces the pool of minority and women candidates, and (3) it reduces career opportunities for criminal justice program graduates who choose professional school over graduate school.

SLOAN T. LETMAN

Letman, S. T. & Spranza, F. G. (1978). "Some sociological perspectives on the immigration problem." *Journal of Humanics* 6(2):107-121.

This article suggests that the wide economic disparity between the United States and Mexico is the source of the illegal alien problem the countries experience. A sociological analysis is conducted focusing on caste, social class and race relations. It is suggested that closing the economic gap between the two countries would be a more useful strategy than attacking the problem directly through police action.

CORAMAE R. MANN

Mann, C. R. (1995). "The contribution of institutionalized racism to minority crime." In *Ethnicity, Race and Crime.* Edited by D.F. Hawkins. Pp. 259-80. Albany: State University of New York Press.

This chapter explores the role that institutionalized racism plays in minority crime and justice in the United States. The racism found in each of the nation's established institutions is enormous, pervasive, and debilitating. At every level of contemporary human existence--education, housing, politics, health, law, welfare, economics, religion, and the family--racism and racial discrimination in American institutions have contributed to and continue to perpetuate the minority status and the current condition of African Americans, Native Americans, Hispanic Americans, and Asian Americans. The author argues that criminal activity, as defined by those in power, may be one of the adaptive responses of racial minorities to institutionalized racism.

Mann, C. R. (1995). "Seventeen white men and me." In *Individual Voices, Collective Visions: Fifty Years of Women in Sociology.* Edited by A. Goetting & S. Fenstermaker (Pp. 273-283). Philadelphia: Temple University Press.

This autobiographical essay discusses the influence of the author's racial and gender status on her life and her scholarship. The realization of being different from the white children she knew, school experiences, encounters with discrimination, community service and years as a professor with seventeen white male colleagues are discussed. The problems of being a black, female academic are highlighted.

Mann, C. R. (1994). "A Minority View of Juvenile Justice." *Washington and Lee Law Review* 51(2):465-478.

This article details the alarming numbers of minority youth being detained in the juvenile justice system. It highlights the "Juvenile Justice and Delinquency Prevention Act" which is designed to, among other things, address the overrepresentation of minorities in the juvenile justice system. The states involved in this legislation, the pilot projects, and the states that are not involved are discussed. Additionally, views about boot camps and juveniles on death row are expressed. Recommendations are offered to institute proper sensitivity training of public servants and a call is made to reconsider some of the measures found in the war on poverty.

Mann, C. R. (1990). "Female homicide and substance use: Is there a connection?" *Women and Criminal Justice* 1(2):87-109.

This article employs official files of females arrested for homicide in six urban areas in 1979 or 1983. A comparison of those who had used alcohol or narcotics prior to the killing (N=96) was made to those who had not (control N=137). An examination of the circumstances surrounding the crimes revealed that alcohol or drug use did not differentiate these subjects. Females who killed tended to be unemployed minority mothers who premeditated the event, whether having used a substance or not. Females who killed also killed alone and claimed little responsibility for the crime.

Mann, C. R. (1990). "Black female homicide in the United States." *Journal of Interpersonal Violence* 5(2):176-201.

A profile of arrested black female homicide offenders was developed using data from random samples of cleared female homicide cases in Chicago, Ill., Houston, Tex., Los Angeles, Calif., and New York City, N.Y. and all female cases in Atlanta, Ga., and Baltimore, Md., for 1979 and 1983. Results show that these offenders kill those closest to them in intersexual, intraracial, intrafamilial homicides. These findings agree with previous research except that, today, guns have replaced knives as the weapon of choice.

ZINA T. MCGEE

Sheley, J.F., **McGee, Z. T.**, & Wright, J. (1995). "Weapon-Related Victimization in Selected Inner-City High School Students." A Final Summary Report Presented to the National Institute of Justice and the Office of Juvenile Justice and Delinquency Prevention, Washington, DC.

National victimization survey data indicate that over two million teenagers are the victims of violent crime annually (U.S. Department of Justice, 1992:28). In addition, numerous studies point to the possession of weapons by adolescents as increasingly problematic. This Summary Report explores the issue of weapon-related victimization of inner-city youths attending high schools with histories of violence. It focuses both on levels of such victimization and on characteristics, settings, and activities-- including participation in illegal behaviors--that might influence victimization status.

Sheley, J.F., **McGee, Z. T.**, & Wright, J. (1992). "Gun-related violence in and around inner-city schools," *American Journal of Diseases of Children* 146(June):677-682.

This article assesses the degree to which inner-city high school students are victimized by threat of or actual firearm attack. A cross-sectional survey was administered to ten inner-city high schools in five cities in four states. A total of 1653 male and female inner-city high school students responded anonymously. Twenty-three percent of respondents were classified as victims. Major variables predicting victimization levels were gender, number of siblings, exposure to violence outside of school, and personal violence-related attributes. Only one in ten victimizations appeared to be random (i.e., not predicted by these variables).

Violence in school is brought into, rather than generated by, the school. Victimized students have characteristics that put them at higher risk of victimization than other students. Given the large number of victimizations and the large number of respondents with risk characteristics, intervention at the individual level seems ineffective. Instead, alteration of community social structure and culture appears to be the appropriate, although difficult, avenue of change for gun-related victimization levels.

McGee, Z. T. (1992). "Social class differences in parental and peer influence on adolescent drug use." *Deviant Behavior: An Interdisciplinary Journal* 13:349-372.

This study uses data extracted from the 1985 version of "Monitoring the Future" to test the hypothesis that the effects of parental and peer influence on adolescent drug use differ significantly by social class. Using variables derived from the social control, social learning, and strain theories of delinquency, strongest support is found for the social learning perspective in that peer influence has the greatest effect on adolescent drug use and the effect of parental influence on adolescent drug use is insignificant. In addition, results show that the effect of parental influence on adolescent drug use is greatest among middle class adolescents. Additional support is found for social control theory in that significant class differences exist with regard to the effects of belief, commitment, religious attachment, and school attachment on adolescent drug use. Finally, results show no support for strain theory in that the effects of expected college success and expected career success on adolescent drug use are insignificant. Implications for integrating the recent work in stratification with the present literature on delinquency are discussed in an effort to provide a more precise explanation of the class-delinquency relationship.

HARVEY L. MCMURRAY

McMurray, H. L. (1993)."High risk parolees in transition from institution to community life." *Journal of Offender Rehabilitation* 19:145-161.

National data indicate that approximately 69% of prisoners aged 25 years and under who are released on parole are re-arrested within three years of their release. Little attention has been given to the transitional process and factors that impact on the adjustment of parolees in their return to community life. This paper reports a study of parolees released in three central North Carolina counties between July 1 and December 31, 1988. Findings indicate that many parolees want a change of lifestyle and report being motivated when released. Community factors (such as discrimination) and individual factors (such as finances, low self-esteem and drug use) appear to hamper successful community adjustment. Parole agency issues are discussed

Leashore, B. R., **McMurray, H. L.** & Bailey, D.C. (1992). "Reuniting and preserving African American families." In *Child Welfare: An Afrocentric Perspective.* Joyce E. Everett, Sandra S. Chipungu, and Bogart R. Leashore (Eds.). (Pp. 247-265). New Brunswick: Rutgers University Press.

Approximately 179,000 children were in foster care or adopted homes in the United States during 1984; nearly 1/3 (32%) of these children were African American; 53% were white, and the remaining 15% were Hispanic or of other racial groups. The plight of African American children in foster care is twofold, i.e., there is a disproportionate number in foster care and they remain longer than their white counterparts. Findings of project VCIN (Volunteers for Children in Need) are presented in this article. A major assumption of the project, conducted through the Howard University School of Social Work in 1985, was that there are untapped community-based resources that could be used to help families with children in foster care. Conducted in Washington, D.C., 98.5% of the children in care were African American. The project emphasizes the need of child welfare policies and practices to focus on strengthening families through the mobilization and utilization of community-based services.

McMurray, H. L. (1990). "Attitudes of assaulted police officers and their policy implications." *Journal of Police Science and Administration* 17:44-48.

Police, particularly those assigned to patrol function, are generally regarded as high-risk candidates for assault. Assaulted officers are said to experience a "second injury"--the first the actual assault, and, the second, the perceived insensitivity from those within the criminal justice system and the community at large. This research project accessed the nature of police post-assault reactions and the buffering effect on personal and work-related social supports. Officers with an official record of their being assaulted between July 1 and December 31, 1986 and who were employed by the Washington, DC (N=77) and the Newark, NJ (N=84) police departments were included. Post-assault attitudes concerning alienation, work-related support, job satisfaction, law enforcement practices are discussed. Comments made by respondents suggest two possible spillover effects on the delivery of police services; they might avoid similar types of situations, or they might become overtly aggressive.

GODPOWER O. OKEREKE

Okereke, G. O. (1993). "Public Attitudes toward the Police Force in Nigeria." *Police Studies* 16(3):113-121.

The attitudes of the Nigerian public towards the Nigerian Police Force is analyzed using data obtained in a 1987 survey (N=116). As expected, the present study found that the Nigerian police force, as well as other oppressive governmental bodies, was viewed unfavorably by the Nigerian public. Reasons for this tend to correspond to widespread perceptions of the excessive use of force. Therefore, changes are needed in both police practices and in their image to improve police and public relations.

SAMPSON IKE OLI

Oli, S. I. (1994). "A dichotomization: Crime and criminality among traditional and Christianized Igbo." In *African American Perspectives on Crime Causation, Criminal Justice Administration, and Crime Prevention.* Edited by Ann T. Sulton. (Pp. 17-32). Englewood, CO: Sulton Books.

This paper examines the social history of the Igbo in Nigeria. Its purpose is to determine the nature and degree of criminality exhibited by the people of this society. Such information will shed light on questions concerning these Africans' involvement in crime as well as in criminal behavior in other countries in which they now reside.

WILLIAM OLIVER

Oliver, W. (1989). "Sexual conquest and patterns of black-on-black violence: A structural-cultural perspective." *Violence and Victims* 4(4):257-273.

This article discusses black-on-black violence in the United States. It summarizes and dismisses several explanations for this problem. An alternative view is presented that emphasizes blacks' dysfunctional adaptations to structural pressures arising from persistent white racism. Dysfunctions include: failure to develop an Afrocentric cultural ideology, adherence of some blacks to "tough guy" and "player of women" image as a masculine ideal. Patterns of violence that arise from these dysfunctions are discussed, and suggestions for future study of the structural-cultural hypothesis are outlined. It is argued that a strong commitment to Afrocentric socialization of black youth can influence success in efforts designed at preventing violence among blacks.

Oliver, W. (1989). "Black males and social problems: Prevention through Afrocentric socialization." *Journal of Black Studies* 20(1):15-39.

Disproportionately high rates of social problems among black males and the causes of these problems are discussed. The article focuses on the interrelationship between structural pressures and dysfunctional cultural adaptations. Specifically, the lack of an internalized Afrocentric worldview and a general tolerance of dysfunctional masculinity orientations have led to the emergence of a cultural context that increases the likelihood of problem behavior. A strategy is proposed which includes: encouragement of the internalization of values that emphasize collectivism, self-love, an increased awareness of cultural heritage, and an increased commitment to the social development of African Americans and other people of African descent.

LEON E. PETTIWAY

Pettiway, L. (1995). "Copping crack: The travel behavior of crack users." *Justice Quarterly* 12(3):499-524.

Considerable attention has been directed to the incidence and distribution of crack in urban areas. In response to public concern about the presence of crack in residential neighborhoods, law enforcement agencies have implemented various law enforcement strategies aimed at reducing or eradicating drugs from urban environments. These strategies, however, have failed to consider crack users' mobility patterns. Because any effort to reduce crack consumption and distribution should consider these patterns, this research assesses the journey to purchase crack and suggests some areas of future research. Initially the research determines how far crack users who travel less than .5 mile on average differ significantly from those who travel more than .5 mile. Moreover, the study explores the influence of socioeconomic factors and characteristics associated with the drug-buying event. Discriminant analysis shows that crack users travel varying distances to purchase the drug. In explaining these differences, gender is an important lifestyle indicator, and the tendency to "cop" in the user's residential neighborhood is a major event characteristic.

Characteristics associated with the crack-buying event are generally more important than individual characteristics in explaining the distances traveled.

Pettiway, L. (1988). "Urban spatial structure and incidence of arson: Differences between ghetto and nonghetto environments." *Justice Quarterly* 5(1):113-29.

This article presents an assessment of arson incidence in ghetto and nonghetto areas of the city of Houston by noting differences in the physical and social composition of the areas. The research assumption is that residential segregation defines and maintains the spatially restricted ghetto in such a way that the ghetto exhibits a spatial structure which differs inherently from that of nonghetto areas. Consequently, different factors may be responsible for the incidence of arson in these two areas. The relative importance of physical or structural variables and of variables that underscore the organization of these communities are used to uncover the differences in arson rates for these two territorial units.

Pettiway, L. (1987). "Participation in crime partnerships by female drug users: The effects of domestic arrangements, drug use, and criminal involvement." *Criminology* 25(3):741-66.

Research findings on the crime patterns of women suggest that social changes in gender roles are associated with increased female criminality. Some researchers note that the increasing participation of women in established criminal organizations increases female crime levels in general. Other researchers demonstrate that involvement with deviant boyfriends or husbands in particular not only introduces women to addictive drugs, but also contributes to greater crime participation. Findings reveal that ethnicity, living with boyfriends or husbands, high levels of crime commission, particularly while carrying weapons, and participating in vice and predatory crimes are factors that are shared by a number of crime partnerships. On the other hand, having children raised by others, a history of incarceration and arrest, and opiate use are factors that are important for specific crime partnerships; therefore, these factors are unique considerations that relate to the likelihood that criminal partnerships will develop.

Pettiway, L. (1987)."Arson for revenge: The role of environmental situation, age, sex and race." *Journal of Quantitative Criminology* 3(2):169-184.

This article analyzes some differences between arson offenses that are expressive (i.e., retaliatory) and those that are instrumental (i.e., nonretaliatory), with a focus on variations in offender characteristics. Loglinear models are constructed using data from the Houston, Texas, fire department of 377 arrested individuals and U.S. census to test the relative effect of individual and neighborhood characteristics on the potential of committing retaliatory or nonretaliatory arson. Age and race differences are revealed as significant, and both are influenced by offender's place of residence. Retaliatory arson is primarily used as a coercive measure or form of conflict management by lower class or dispossessed individuals for whom the function of the law has failed.

ERNEST QUIMBY

Quimby, E. (1995). "Homeless clients' perspectives on recovery in the Washington, DC, dual diagnosis project." *Contemporary Drug Problems* 22(2):265-289.

Dually diagnosed homeless adults require integrated services that can provide substance abuse care, mental health treatment, housing, health care and social support. This paper examines the Washington, DC, Dual Diagnosis Project from 1990-1993. Clinical records and interviews provided ethnographic data from 50 dually diagnosed homeless persons. Findings suggest that service delivery which incorporates clients' perspectives while addressing their interrelated mental health and drug abuse problems enhances substance abuse treatment.

Quimby, E. (1993). "Obstacles to reducing AIDS among African Americans." *Journal of Black Psychology* 19(2):215-222.

This article attempts to determine the major obstacles hindering the sustenance of African American mobilization efforts against AIDS. Objective conditions, perceptions of substance abuse and AIDS/HIV, attitudes toward sexuality and conflicting policy views are discussed. Institutional responses to the disease occur within circumstances of perceived oppression, neglect, competing agendas, and religious conservatism. Inadequate public health education, lack of systematized or comprehensive efforts, suspicion, public fear, and misinformation also contribute to impaired mobilization. Many efforts have been top-down actions carried out by professionals aimed at their constituencies instead of African American neighborhoods. Finally, risky behaviors of drug addicts and their sex partners have been insufficiently dissuaded.

Quimby, E. (1990). "Drug trafficking and the Caribbean connection: Survival mechanisms, entrepreneurship and social symptoms." *Urban League Review* 14(2):61-70.

This article argues that the development of effective solutions to the drug problem have been hindered by stereotypical images that criminalize Caribbean youth, especially Jamaicans. These images overshadow the systemic social inequalities of which drug trafficking and abuse are symptoms. The relationship between drug trafficking and underdevelopment is explored through ethnographic (observation and informal) interviews during 1986-1988 in ethnic neighborhoods of the New York City area. Findings confirm that Caribbean drug trafficking is a survival strategy, and viable solutions to this problem must address the social inequalities that foster its necessity.

LEE E. ROSS

Ross, L. E. (1996). "The relationship between religion, self-esteem, and delinquency." *Journal of Crime and Justice* 19(2):195-214.

The impact of religious and self-esteem factors on delinquency has received considerable attention. Despite significant contributions, however, few studies have explored whether the combined effects of religion and self-esteem influence crime/delinquency. The present study examines (a) whether religion, self-esteem, and delinquency are interrelated, and (b) whether the interaction of religion and self-esteem, as well as the main effects of these factors, affects delinquency. Through an examination of 15 ordinary least squares (OLS) regression models, the findings are twofold: (a) main effects of religion and self-esteem affect certain forms of delinquency, and (b) the combined effects of religion and self-esteem do not affect delinquency. The implications of these findings are discussed.

Ross, L. E. (1995). "School environment, self-esteem, and delinquency." *Journal of Criminal Justice* 23(6):555-567.

The positive and negative effects of one's school environment (and interracial contact within this environment) have been widely debated. A question of great concern is whether the racial composition (e.g., school environment) of a school affects one's self-esteem. The present study explored whether self-esteem, race-esteem, school commitment, and delinquency differ by the racial composition of a school. Self-report questionnaires were administered to a random sample of 1,100 high school students in a large Midwestern city of the United States. The findings (a) suggest that all four measures differ by school environment, and (b) provide partial support for earlier studies claiming that, within racially homogeneous school environments, African American students, in particular, enjoy higher self-esteem. Moreover, this finding might suggest that racial diversity within certain school environments (e.g., mostly Caucasian or equally mixed) carries with it lower levels of self-esteem. Higher rates of self-reported delinquency, however, were found in the equally mixed school environment than in racially homogeneous school environments.

Ross, L. E. (1994). "The impact of race-esteem and self-esteem on delinquency." *Sociological Focus* 27(2):111-129.

This article presents findings from a study of the relationships between race, self-esteem and delinquency. Of major concern was whether personal measures of self-esteem correlated with group measures of self-esteem, and more importantly, whether either measure affects delinquency. Self-report questionnaires were administered to a random sample of 1,100 high school students from Milwaukee, Wisconsin. Scales of self-esteem and delinquency were factor analyzed. It was discovered that factors representing personal identity measures of self-esteem were almost identical for both races. However, there were racial differences in the relationships between factors of self-esteem and delinquency. Multiple regression analyses revealed that for blacks both personal and group measures of self-esteem are related to delinquency. For whites, however, personal identity measures of self-esteem are better predictors of delinquency than are group measures. The implications of these findings are discussed.

Ross, L. E. (1994). "Religion and deviance: Exploring the impact of social control elements." *Sociological Spectrum* (14):65-86.

This study explored, from a social control perspective, the relationships between religiosity and various acts of self-reported deviance. As an extension of social control theory, this study sought to assess the importance of religion relative to other forms of social control in explaining deviance. In doing so, unidimensional and multidimensional measures of religiosity were employed. Findings from this study are twofold: (1) In the regression model, neither multidimensional measures nor unidimensional measures of religiosity are significant variables for explaining variance in self-reported deviance; and (2) The significant variables were moral beliefs, family attachment, and respect for authority. If religion affects deviance, it might do so indirectly. This highlights a need to employ advanced research methodologies and statistical techniques that are capable of clarifying the path of religiosity in impacting deviance.

Ross, L. E. (1992). "Blacks, self-esteem, and delinquency: It's time for a new approach." *Justice Quarterly* 9(4):609-624.

For decades, sociology and social psychology have debated the nature of self-esteem and its role in determining behavior. More recently, race has been added to the mixture, as social scientists have sought to explain black self-esteem and the involvement of black youth in delinquency. The article reviews a number of studies to explore the relative importance of race as an explanatory factory. Questions of the validity of prior measures of self-esteem are raised, especially where racial comparisons of self-esteem and delinquency were made. This article identifies various conceptual and methodological problems inherent to studies of race, self-esteem, and delinquency. In doing so, distinctions are made among personal and group identity measures of self-esteem in an effort to further the cause of research in this area.

KATHERYN RUSSELL

Russell, K. (1996). "The racial hoax as crime: The law as affirmation." *Indiana Law Journal* 71(3):594-621.

This article chronicles the number of racial hoaxes (e.g., Susan Smith, Charles Stuart cases) and argues that they should be made criminal offenses. Specifically, the article examines the sociology of the racial hoax, how it affects Blacks and Whites. The article sets forth components of a racial hoax law and assesses the societal costs of failure to adopt such a law.

Russell, K. (1994). "A critical view from the inside: An application of critical legal studies to criminal law and criminology." *Journal of Criminal Law and Criminology* 85(1):222-40.

Critical Legal Studies (CLS) provides a theoretical critique of the law in operation. To date, very few CLS analyses have focused upon criminal law. This phenomenon is particularly glaring given the prominence of criminal law in the American judicial system. This article provides an overview of the CLS movement and a discussion of the value of deconstructing criminal law cases. Four legal formalisms are then used to critique the *McCleskey v. Kemp* decision. A fifth formalism, the "sociology of race relations" is offered and applied to critique McCleskey.

Russell, K. (1994). "The racial inequality hypothesis: A critical look at the research and an alternative theoretical analysis." *Law and Human Behavior* 18(3):305-17.

The author reviews and critiques the racial inequality hypothesis. Following a review of theory, empirical findings and underlying premises, the value of racial inequality as a measure of economic inequality is assessed. An alternative measure of racial inequality is assessed and presented, one that attempts to measure this concept as independent from economic inequality.

Russell, K. (1994). "The constitutionality of jury override in Alabama death penalty cases." *Alabama Law Review* 46(1):5-45.

This article examines Alabama jury override, a system which permits a judge in death penalty cases to override the jury's decision to sentence a defendant to life without parole and impose the death penalty. Jury override operates in four states. The article provides an empirical and legal analysis of how Alabama judges utilize jury override.

Russell, K. (1992). "Development of a Black criminology and the role of the Black criminologist." *Justice Quarterly* 9(4):667-84.

In its study of Black criminality, the discipline of criminology has failed to cultivate a cohesive, continuous and recognized body of research--what is termed a "Black criminology." Inasmuch as the theoretical framework of the discipline is limited by its failure to develop this subfield, policy recommendations proposed to and adopted by the criminal justice system are limited. It is argued that the development of a Black criminology is necessary to fill this gap--much in the same way that feminist criminology filled a void. The components and scope of this subfield are outlined and the role of the Black criminologist in the development of a Black criminology is evaluated. It is argued that although Black criminologists are needed to chart a Black criminology, their participation alone is insufficient for the full development and vitality of this subfield.

ELSIE SCOTT

Scott, E. (1994). "Reducing the involvement of African American males in the criminal justice system." In *African American Perspectives on Crime Causation, Criminal Justice Administration, and Crime Prevention.* Edited by Ann T. Sulton. (Pp. 185-200). Englewood, CO: Sulton Books.

This article focuses on the overrepresentation of African American males in the criminal justice system. While acknowledging the potential for alternatives to incarceration, the author sees a review of factors outside the criminal justice system as necessary for an understanding of why African American males are overrep-resented. The article presents a number of policy recom-mendations and actions that can be implemented by governmental agencies, private industry, community and national organizations, and individuals to reduce the involvement of African American males in the criminal justice system. Included among the recommendations are: (1) greater emphasis on education, including anti-drop out policies, (2) using federal and state governments to develop comprehensive job training programs, (3) seeking federal legislation requiring registration of all handguns, and (4) encouraging law enforcement agencies to adopt policies restricting the use of deadly force.

Scott, E. (1975). "Black attitudes toward crime and crime prevention." In *Crime and Its Impact on the Black Community*. Edited by L.E. Gary and L.P. Brown. (Pp. 13-30). Washington, DC: Howard University Institute for Urban Affairs and Research.

In her presentation, the author examines the attitudes of Blacks toward crime in their community, crime victimization, and police and citizen crime prevention efforts. Her analysis resulted from surveys of professionals, non-professionals, students, and others. Findings suggests that personal crime was nearly triple the rate of reported property crime. Among victims who reported to the police, less than nine percent responded that a subsequent arrest occurred. Thirty-two percent reported that the police did absolutely nothing. Overall, respondents' support for the concept of vigilante groups suggests a lack of faith in the police to control crime on the local level.

PHILLIP E. SECRET

Johnson, J. B. & **Secret, P. E.** (1995). "The effects of court structure on juvenile court decisionmaking." *Journal of Criminal Justice* 23(1):63-82.

This article examines the differences in adjudications (delinquent or dismissal) and final dispositions (transfers of custody or no transfer of custody) of specialized juvenile courts compared to courts of general jurisdiction hearing cases involving juvenile defendants. The data are from juvenile court records of the state of Nebraska for 1982 through 1987. The study uses logistic regression to examine the differences in the behavior of the two types of courts while controlling for extralegal, legal, and county environmental characteristics of the defendants. The authors found statistically significant differences in the adjudication decisions but not in the final dispositions of the two kinds of courts. The findings are discussed within the framework of the "parens patriae" philosophy.

Secret, P. E. & Johnson, J. B. (1989). "Racial difference in attitudes toward crime control." *Journal of Criminal Justice* 17:361-375.

This research examined the connection between race and attitudes toward crime. Using simple cross tabulation, the authors looked for racial differences in attitudes toward court harshness, use of wiretaps, support of gun control, and government spending to control crime and drug use. Hierarchical multiple regression analysis was used to discover the extent that race, rather than socioeconomic, sociological, political, or demographic variables, explains differences between the attitudes of blacks and whites toward crime. Differences in reported gun ownership were also researched. The authors found some convergence between attitudes of blacks and whites toward crime since 1980. Bivariate analysis found statistically significant differences between the attitudes of blacks and whites for all dependent variables. But in the multivariate analysis, race was a significant factor only on attitudes toward court harshness and use of wiretaps once other factors were controlled. Theoretical and policy implications are discussed.

LARRY D. STOKES

Stokes, L. D. & Scott, J.F. (1996). "Affirmative action and selected minority groups in law enforcement." *Journal of Criminal Justice* 24(1):29-38.

This study examines the political controversy surrounding affirmative action and race norming, as well as the extent to which minority groups are represented in nineteen municipal police departments in the United States. Unequivocally, there have been increases of minority members among sworn officers in law enforcement agencies since the 1968 report of the National Advisory Commission on Civil Disorders. The future has been clouded, however, by the recent decision in *Adarand Constructors v. Pena* (115 S.Ct. 1841, 1995), the 1991 Civil Rights Act, the Republican assault upon affirmative action, and President Clinton's equivocation. In lieu of the *Adarand* decision, the legitimization of the police role is often contingent upon how the police are viewed relative to a community's racial, ethnic, and gender composition.

Stokes, L. D. & Venters, K. (1993). "Black homicide in a midsize southern city, 1980-1989." *American Journal of Criminal Justice* 17(2):61-71.

This study examined homicides from 1980-1989 in a midsize southern city (Chattanooga, Tennessee). More specifically, the study examined the homicide rate as it related to age, gender, and race of both the victim and offender, as well as the type of weapon used.

ANNE T. SULTON

Sulton, A. T. (1994). "Preventing crime through economic development in urban neighborhoods." In *African American Perspectives on Crime Causation, Criminal Justice Administration, and Crime Prevention*. Edited by A.T. Sulton. (pp. 201-22). Englewood, CO: Sulton Books.

This article provides a scathing critique of both criminological theory and current efforts to control crime (especially within urban neighborhoods). The author regards such efforts as too often based on either emotional responses to criminal incidents, personal opinion, and/or political expediency. Furthermore, the author argues that more law enforcement is not the answer, adding that those who advocate mechanical and punitive measures can offer little concrete evidence of the viability of such approaches to crime. To address problems of crime, the author asserts that the criminal justice system is in dire need of a carefully thought-out, long term plan that builds on our nation's strengths. Small businesses are identified as one of those strengths. They enable job creation in urban neighborhoods and job creation holds the greatest promise for preventing crime.

Sulton, A. T. (ed.). (1994). *African American Perspectives on Crime Causation, Criminal Justice Administration, and Crime Prevention.* Englewood, CO: Sulton Books.

This edited work consists of a collection of articles, authored by leading African American criminologists and practitioners. Included within these articles are many recommendations that, if implemented, might lead to a reduction in crime. The articles present fresh and exciting new ways of thinking about a wide variety of contemporary crime problems. Read together, as a whole, they provide a partially completed blueprint for a safer and more just society. Included among the featured African American criminologists and practitioners are: Charisse Coston, David Fattah, Laura Fishman, Helen Taylor-Greene, Sampson Ike Oli, Lee E. Ross, Elsie Scott, Charles R. See, Becky Tatum, Dorothy Taylor, and Vernetta Young.

BECKY L. TATUM

Tatum, B. L. (1996). "An analysis of factors contributing to the delinquency of the black youth." *Journal of Black Studies* 26(3):356-368.

This study examines the relationship between nine economic and demographic characteristics of 57 New York state counties and black and white juvenile arrest rates. The study argues that in comparison to whites: (1) black delinquency rates can be explained by economic factors and that (2) unemployment rates (both adult and juvenile) have a greater impact upon black delinquency than social or demographic variables. Findings suggest that juvenile arrest rates are not affected by economic characteristics but are dependent upon whether the county is urban (where blacks compose the majority of the population) or rural (where whites compose the majority of the population). Because of the lack of residential variability in New York state counties, the author suggests that city-level rather than county-level data may provide a better unit of analysis.

Tatum, B. L. (1994). "The colonial model as a theoretical explanation of crime and delinquency." In *African American Perspectives on Crime Causation, Criminal Justice Administration, and Crime Prevention.* Edited by A.T. Sulton. (Pp. 33-52). Englewood, CO: Sulton Books.

This chapter reviews the original version of the colonial model and the application of internal colonialism to the United States. The adequacy of internal colonialism in explaining the relationship between race and crime is also addressed.

DOROTHY L. TAYLOR

Taylor, D. L. & Bing, R.L. (1995). "Racial discrimination in the juvenile justice system: Some unanswered questions." *Challenge* 6(2):5-28.

This article reviews the empirical literature on the role of race in the processing of juvenile offenders at every stage of the juvenile justice system. In general and specific comments, it points to the contradictions between research findings and policies, discusses the failure to implement the *Gault* decision, and stresses the need to consider the entire system as a process. In addition, it urges the use of a multistage research approach in future studies of various aspects of this issue.

Taylor, D. L. (1994) "Family and Delinquency: African American Female Headed Households and Chronic Maladaptive Behavior of Juveniles." In *African American Perspectives on Crime Causation, Criminal Justice Administration, and Crime Prevention.* Edited by Ann T. Sulton. (Pp. 124-38). Englewood, CO: Sulton Books.

The existing literature on African American female-headed households devotes little attention to the interaction between the parent and the child, and on whether this interaction contributes to or deters the development of the child's maladaptive behavior. This paper addresses this issue. The present study was designed to determine the relationships between female-headed households and juvenile maladaptive behavior by exploring interpersonal bonding factors related to parent-child relationships. The importance of this study is that it challenges the myth that children from female-headed African American families are destructive and dysfunctional. Quite the contrary. Moreover, the findings provide additional empirical support for social control theories and suggest new directions for future research.

Taylor, D. L., Chitwood, D.D., McElrath, K., & Belgrave, L.L. (1994). "Ethnicity, social support, and injection drug use." *Journal of Black Psychology* 20(1):36-46.

There is considerable agreement that the prevalence of diagnosed AIDS cases and the prevalence of HIV infection is greater among African American and Hispanic injection drug users (IDUs) than among Anglo (White, non-Hispanic) IDUs. There is less agreement on why this in the case. This lack of knowledge is related, in part, to the paucity of research on the cultural diversity among IDUs and the impact that cultural differences have on infection risk behaviors of those three groups. This analysis examined possible differences in the sources from which each ethnic group obtained their works (IV equipment) in a sample of 711 infecting drug users drawn from six methadone clinics, three residential treatment programs, and one drug detoxification program between June 1987 and August 1988 in South Florida. It was found that African Americans were more likely (69.4%) to acquire their works from street suppliers than were Hispanics (49.4%) or Anglos (36.1%). It is conceivable that "source of works" is a contributing factor to the higher prevalence of AIDS among minority IDUs.

MARIAN WHITSON

Whitson, M. & Moyer, I. (1994) "Patriarchy, power differentials, and women offenders." In I.L. Moyer (Ed.), *The Changing Role of Women in the Criminal Justice System*, 2nd Edition. (Pp. 31-56). Prospect Heights, IL: Waveland Press.

This chapter examines the changing role of women offenders as presented by historians and researchers over the last two centuries. The authors demonstrate that interest in women has concerned two types of women offenders, mainly prostitutes and murderers. They further demonstrate that views of women offenders differ from that of mainstream scholars and that considerable attention is devoted to minority offenders. The authors argue that feminist theory and research must be accepted and integrated as an essential part of mainstream criminology.

JIMMY J. WILLIAMS

Williams, J. J. (1995). "Type of counsel and the outcome of criminal appeals: A research note." *American Journal of Criminal Justice* 19(2):

Previous studies have focused on type of counsel and case outcome at trial court, but only a few have done so at the appellate level. The purpose of this research note is to provide some insight into the influence of type of counsel on the outcome of criminal appeals. Results indicate that in criminal appeals from two Florida trial courts to an intermediate appellate court type of counsel was nonsignificant in predicting the court's decision. The implications of the findings are discussed.

Williams, J. J. (1995). "Race of appellant, sentencing guidelines, and decisionmaking in criminal appeals: A research note." *Journal of Criminal Justice* 23(1):83-91.

Many studies have examined race and the processing of criminal cases at trial court. Practically no studies exist on race and decisionmaking in criminal appeals. This research note explores the influence of race on decisions reached in criminal appeals from two Florida trial courts to an intermediate appellate court. The results indicate that African American appellants who had been sentenced in excess of the recommended maximum sentence were more likely to have the trial court's decision affirmed on appeal. The implications of the findings of the study also are discussed.

Williams, J. J. (1994). "Controlling the Judge's Discretion: Appellate Review of Departures Made in Sentencing Guideline Cases." *The Justice System Journal* 17(2):229-240.

The purpose of this study is to determine the extent and under what circumstances an intermediate appellate court is likely to disagree with trial judges' decisions in guideline appeals. Results indicate that in most appeals, the appellate court did not challenge trial judges' use of discretion in guideline appeals. However, results indicate that the appellate court was inconsistent in its decisions in which trial judges cited invalid reasons for departing from recommended sentences. The implications of the results are also discussed.

Williams, J. J. (1992). "Sentencing guidelines and the changing composition of criminal appeals: A preliminary analysis." *Judicature* 76(2):94-96.

After sentencing guidelines were enacted in Florida, the number of criminal appeals in two sample counties remained constant. The appellate court reached decisions faster in guilty plea appeals, which became predominant, than in jury trial appeals.

Williams, J. J. (1991). "Predicting Decisions Rendered in Criminal Appeals." *Journal of Criminal Justice* 19:463-469.

This study examined whether select legal and extra-legal factors were significant in predicting the decisions rendered in criminal appeals from two trial courts to an intermediate appellate court in Florida. Mode of disposition at trial court and the type of counsel who filed the appeal were insignificant, whereas the race of the defendant and whether the trial judge departed from the sentence recommended by the guidelines were significant. It is suggested future studies focus on legal and extralegal factors as predictors of decisions in criminal appeals.

GEORGE P. WILSON

Wilson, G. P., & McMurray, H. L. (1990). *Durham County Jail Population Management Plan.* Durham, NC: UNCC Department of Criminal Justice.

Overcrowding at the Durham County Jail has resulted in the threat of federal litigation to improve inmate conditions. To enhance plans for the overall management of the jail population, the Durham County Manager initiated the Jail Population Management Project to develop assumptions believed to affect jail overcrowding. These assumptions were refined; tested using jail, court and law enforcement data; validated where applicable; and ultimately paired with recommendations for management actions, policies and programs. This jail population management plan represents a continuing effort to address the problem of jail overcrowding.

Wilson, G. P., Cullen, F. T., Latessa, E. J. & Wills, J.S. (1985). "State Intervention and Victimless Crimes: A Study of Police Attitudes" *Journal of Police Science and Administration* 13(1):22-29.

This article seeks to improve our understanding of how officers stand on the control of crimes without victims. Based on a survey of a department located in a Midwestern city, the following were examined: 1) general attitudes of officers toward state legal intervention, 2) attitudes toward the use of the criminal justice system to combat specific types of victimless offenses, and 3) how attitudes were shaped by characteristics of the officers sampled. Findings indicate that the officers sampled do not view vice as a serious problem, see no public mandate to increase their current surveillance procedures, and have a tendency to believe that it is futile to try to control victimless crimes.

Wilson, G. P. (1983). "Halfway House Programs for Offenders." *Probation, Parole, and Community Corrections: A Reader.* Edited by Lawrence F. Travis III. (pp. 151-164). Prospect Heights, IL: Waveland Press.

The continued growth of the Community-Based-Corrections ideal and the utilization of halfway houses for criminal offenders is a rather recent phenomenon. However, criminal justice and correctional administrators have erroneously assumed that the development of halfway houses for criminal offenders was a by-product of the rehabilitation era as opposed to previous eras of punishment and deterrence. A close examination of the historical development of the United States halfway house will suggest the inaccuracy of this assumption.

BENJAMIN S. WRIGHT

Wright, B. S. & Senese, J. D. (1996). "An analysis of selected aspects of police training." *Journal of Contemporary Criminal Justice* 12(3):235-49.

The present study attempts to determine if the retention of police in-service training information is affected by the type of content presented in the training session. A group of mid-level police managers (e.g., mostly lieutenants) attended two in-service training sessions on the same day that were devoted to Personnel Management and Multicultural Police Strategies. The police managers were given three objective tests related to the content of the two training sessions. Through the use of an experimental design the police managers were administered a pre-test immediately before each training session; a post-test immediately following each training session; and a second post-test three months after the completion of the training sessions. These objective tests focused on both perceptions of information retained as well as the ability to demonstrate actual knowledge in the two training areas. The results show that there were significant differences in the perceptions of police information retention across the two contents, but there were no differences in demonstrated knowledge. Recommendations for future research on police training involve improving the panel design and broadening the training content focus.

Wright, B. S. (1993) "An examination of gender issues that were observed in the proportion of arrests over time." In *Female Criminality: The State of the Art.* Edited by C.C. Culliver. (Pp. 305-20). New York: Garland Publishing.

Thus far, few investigations have addressed variations in the arrest rate on the basis of gender and race influences. Among studies that have investigated gender differences at the arrest stage, the findings have not only contradicted previous research but have made interpretation difficult. This study attempts to determine if there were time-related gender differences in the proportion of male and female arrests for Uniform Crime Report Part I offenses (except for arson and larceny-theft). The difference-in-means test was used to analyze gender variation for each of the eight time positions under investigation. Findings suggest that males consistently had a greater involvement in all six index offenses than did females. Also of interest is that female involvement decreased for the time periods 1965-70, 1975-80, and 1980-85. The implications of the findings are discussed.

Wright, B. S., Doerner, W.G., & Speir, J.C. (1990). "Pre-employment psychological testing as a predictor of police performance during an FTO program." *American Journal of Police* 9(4):65-83.

The present study began by examining whether the Minnesota Multiphasic Personality Inventory (MMPI) and the California Personality Inventory (CPI) could predict Behaviorally Anchored

Rating Scale (BARS) measures of police performance during the initial Field Training Officer (FTO) program. The results indicate a virtual lack of a relationship. While such findings are disheartening, they are consistent with studies using subjective and objective measures of police performance. As a result, the authors suggest a need to reshape the psychological component of the police selection process. One possible alternative is the adoption of the Inwald Personality Inventory (IPI) which has shown promise when coupled with subjective and objective indicators of police performance. What is needed now is an examination of the IPI with respect to law enforcement BARS measures, before it can replace other psychological screening devices.

Doerner, W. G., Speir, J. C., & **Wright, B. S.** (1989). "An analysis of rater-ratee race and sex influences upon field training officer program evaluations." *Journal of Criminal Justice* 17(2): 103-114.

One recent innovation in law enforcement is the implementation of field training officer (FTO) programs. The FTO program is a post-academy training period during which candidates receive additional instruction and have their field performance monitored on a daily basis. Black and female trainees in general receive lower scores than whites and males in the agency under study. Given differential success rates, the question becomes whether ratee and rater characteristics, such as race and sex, influence evaluations. An analysis of training scores from an FTO program in one south-eastern municipal police agency indicated that rater characteristics do not alter ratee scores. Despite the introduction of a uniform program with a standardized rating format, these results pinpoint a program deficiency and suggest the need for a more structured instructional format in order to balance trainee success rates.

VERNETTA YOUNG

Young, V. & Greene, H.T. (1995). "Pedagogical Reconstruction:

Incorporating African American Perspectives into the Curriculum."
Journal of Criminal Justice Education. 6(1):85-104.

This article seeks to analyze historical and contemporary works by African Americans on race and crime, and to begin integrating these works into the criminal justice/criminology curriculum. In doing so, African American perspectives are discussed in the context of the ongoing cultural/multicultural debate. Since the turn of the century, African American scholars have examined race and crime in a social, economic, and practical context. Unfortunately, most of these works have not filtered into mainstream criminology/criminal justice, and are omitted from textbooks and classroom discussion. Moreover, African American contributions have been largely ignored. By way of addressing these concerns, the authors recommend strategies for incorporating these materials into existing undergraduate and graduate courses.

Young, V. (1994). "The politics of disproportionality." In *African American Perspectives on Crime Causation, Criminal Justice Administration, and Crime Prevention.* Edited by Ann T. Sulton. (pp. 69-81). Englewood, CO: Sulton Books.

This article traces the long and varied history of the counting of Blacks in America. It contends that over the last two hundred years the nature and objectives of these approaches to the counting of Blacks have been novel. This article examines these approaches to determine the functions they have served in the measurement of Blacks in America. The objective was to explore the use of the concept of disproportionality as it relates race and crime. Conclusions suggest that the concept of diproportionality has been used adversely against Black offenders. Moreover, it has been used to identify the Black male as a "typical criminal." Consequently, it has served to divert attention away from non-Black offenders involved in serious crime. The author advises that our definition (and concept) of crime must be extended beyond that of "street crime."

Young, V. & Sulton, A. T. (1991). "Excluded: The current status of African American scholars in the field of criminology and criminal justice." *Journal of Research in Crime and Delinquency.* 28:101-16.

The contributions of African American criminologists to the study of crime and justice have been virtually ignored. The failure to include African American perspectives on crime coupled with a continued neglect of their views on criminal justice policy and the lack of an African American presence on editorial boards of major journals lead these authors to conclude that African American criminologists are intentionally excluded. In contrast, ideas advanced by white criminologists have assumed prominent positions in the field of criminology. This article represents an initial step toward quickening the pace of progress. The authors' primary objective is to encourage policymakers to include the perspectives advanced by African American criminologists.

Selected References

Agozino, B. (1996). "Football and the civilizing process: Penal discourse and the ethic of collective responsibility in sports law." *International Journal of the Sociology of Law* 24(2):163-88.

Agozino, B. (1995). "Radical criminology in African literature." *International Sociology Association* 10(3):315-29.

Agozino, B. (1977). *Black Women and the Criminal Justice System: Towards the Decolonisation of Victimization.* Avebury: Aldershot.

Austin, R. L. (1993) "Recent trends in official male and female crime rates: The convergence controversy." *Journal of Criminal Justice* 21(5):447-88.

Austin, R. L. & Arthur J. (1992). "Family disruption, violent victimization and protest masculinity." *International Review of Victimology* 2(2):103-25.

Austin, R. L. (1992) "Race, female headship, and delinquency: A longitudinal analysis." *Justice Quarterly* 9(2):585-607

Austin, R. L. & Stack, S. (1988). "Race, class, and opportunity: Changing realities and perceptions." *Sociological Quarterly* 29(3):357-69.

Austin, R. L. (1982). "Women's liberation and increases in minor, major, and occupational offenses." *Criminology* 20(3 &4):407-30.

Austin, R. L. (1981). "Liberation and female criminality in England and Wales." *British Journal of Criminology* 21(4):371-374.

Austin, R. L. (1980). "Adolescent subcultures of violence." *The Sociological Quarterly* 21(Autumn):545-61.

Austin, R. L. (1978). "Race, father-absence, and female delinquency." *Criminology* 15(4):487-504.

Austin, R. L. (1977). "Differential treatment in an institution: Reexamining the Preston Study." *Journal of Research in Crime and Delinquency* (July):177-194.

Bailey, F. (1996). "The tangle of pathology and the lower class African American family: Historical and social science perspectives." In *Justice with Prejudice: Race and Criminal Justice in America.* Edited by M.J. Lynch and E.B. Patterson. (Pp. 49-71). New York: Harrow and Heston.

Bailey, F. (1993). "Getting Justice: Real Life Vigilantism and Vigilantism in Popular Films." *The Justice Professional.* 8(1):33-51.

Bailey, F. (1991). "Law, justice and Americans: An historical overview." In *Justice with Prejudice: Race and Criminal Justice.* Edited by M. J. Lynch, and E. B. Patterson. (Pp. 10-21). New

York: Harrow and Heston.

Duffee, D.E. & **Bailey, F.** (1991). "A criminal justice contribution to a general education diversity requirement." *Journal of Criminal Justice Education* 2(1):141-157.

Bing, R. L., Heard, C.A., & Gilbert, E. (1995). "The experiences of African Americans and whites in criminal justice education: Do race and gender differences exist?" *Journal of Criminal Justice Education* 4(1):123-41.

Taylor, D.L. & **Bing, R. L.** (1995). "Racial discrimination in the juvenile justice system: Some unanswered questions." *Challenge* 6(2):5-28.

Bing, R. L., & Harvey-Holmes, P. (1993). "Does race make a difference in the reporting of crime? A research note." *Journal of Research on Minority Affairs* 4(1):11-15.

Bing, R. L. (1992). "Politicizing black-on-black crime: A critique of terminological preference." *Journal of Research on Minority Affairs* 3(1):33-41.

Bing, R. L. (1991). "Fines and fines administration: Can the private sector fill the void?" *Judicature* 75(1):5, 50.

Brown. L. (1977). "Bridges over troubled waters: A perspective on policing in the black community." In *Black Perspectives on Crime and the Criminal Justice System.* Edited by R.L. Woodson. Pp. 79-106. Boston: Hall.

Brown, L. (1975) "New directions in law enforcement." In *Crime and its impact on the black community.* Edited by L.E. Gary and L.P. Brown. Pp. 143-54. Washington, DC: Howard University Institute for Urban Affairs and Research.

Brown, L. (1974). "The impact of crime and the criminal justice system on the Black community: An overview." In *Social Research and the Black Community: Selected Issues and Priorities.* Edited by L.E. Gary. (Pp. 88-98). Washington, DC: Howard University Institute for Urban Affairs and Research.

Brown, L. (1974). "The Police and Higher Education: The Challenge of the Times." *Criminology*, 12(1):114-124.

Browning, S. L. & Cao, L. (1992). "The impact of race on criminal justice ideology." *Justice Quarterly.* 9(4):685-701.

Nalla, M.K. & **Corley, C. J.** (1996). "Race and criminal justice: Employment of minorities in the criminal justice field." In *Justice with Prejudice: Race and Criminal Justice in America.* Edited by M.J. Lynch and E.B. Patterson. (Pp. 139-55). New York: Harrow and Heston.

Wordes, M., Bynum, T. S., & **Corley, C. J.** (1996). "Locking up youth: The impact of race on detention decisions." *Journal of Research in Crime and Delinquency* 31(2):149-65.

Corley, C. J., Bynum, T.S., & Wordes, M. (1995). "Conceptions of family and juvenile court processes: A qualitative assessment." *The Justice System Journal* 18(2):157-172.

Payne, D.M. & **Corley, C. J.** (1994). "Police pursuits: Correlates of the failure to report." *American Journal of Police* 13(4):47-72.

Corley, C. J. & Woods, A.Y. (1991). "Socioeconomic, socio-demographic and attitudinal correlates of the tempo of divorce." *Journal of Divorce and Remarriage* 16(1/2):47-68.

Coston, C. T. & Finckenauer, J.O. (1993). "Fear of crime among vulnerable populations: Homeless women." *Journal of Social Distress and the Homeless* 2(1):1-21.

Coston, C. T. (1989). "The original designer label: Prototypes of

New York City's shopping-bag ladies." *Deviant Behavior* 10(2):157-172.

Coston, C. T. (1993). "Worries about crime: Rank ordering survival concerns among urban transient females." *Deviant Behavior: An Interdisciplinary Journal* 14:365-376.

Coston, C. T. (1992). "The influence of race in urban homeless females' fear of crime." *Justice Quarterly* 9(4):721-30.

Helal, A.A. and **Coston, C. T.** (1991). "Low crime rates in Bahrain: Islamic social control--testing the theory of Synnomie." In *Comparative Criminal Justice's Traditional and Non-Traditional Systems of Law and Control*. Charles Fields and Richter Moore (eds.), New York: Waveland Press.

Debro, J. & Conley, D. (1993). "School and Community Politics: Issues, Concerns, and Implications when Conducting Research in African American Communities." *NIDA Research Monograph, #30, U.S. Department of Health and Human Services*.

Debro, J. (1989). "Homicide in Black communities: A public health perspective." *Ethnicity and Health* 7:179-201.

Debro, J., Murty, K.S., and Bonds, T. (1986). "Does income affect crime? An empirical analysis of Black communities in Atlanta, Ga." *Journal of Southern Society of Economics* 13(1):1-12.

Debro, J. (1977). "Institutional racism within the structure of American prisons." In *Black Perspectives on Crime and the Criminal Justice System*. Edited by R.L. Woodson. (Pp. 143-60). Boston: Hall.

Debro, J. (1974). "Perspectives on blacks in the correctional process." In *Social Research and the Black Community: Selected Issues and Priorities*. Edited by L.E. Gary. (Pp. 105-111). Washington, DC: Howard University Press.

Debro, J. (1974). "The Black offender as victim." *Journal of Afro-American Issues.* 2:149-66.

Debro, J. (1973). "Black lawyers in the bay area and the Black community." *Journal of Social and Behavioral Sciences,* Summer-Fall, 13-26.

Dorsey, R. R., & Giacopassi, D.J. (1987). "Demographics and work-related correlates of police officer cynicism." In *Police and Law Enforcement.* Edited by D. B. Kennedy and R. J Homant. (Pp. 173-88). New York: AMS Press, Inc.

Dorsey, R. R. & Giacopassi, D. J. (1986). "Assessing gender differences in the levels of cynicism among police officers." *American Journal of Police* 5(1):91-112.

Ebbie, O. (1992). "Juvenile delinquency in Nigeria: The problem of application of Western theories." *International Journal of Comparative and Applied Criminal Justice* 16(2):353-370.

Ebbie, O. (1990). "Heads of state: The vice kings and narcotic barons." *International Journal of Comparative and Applied Criminal Justice* 14(2):112-124.

Ebbie, O. (1988). "Juvenile justice system in southern Nigeria." *International Journal of Comparative and Applied Criminal Justice* 12(2):83-95.

Ebbie, O. (1985). "The correlates of female criminality in Nigeria." *International Journal of Comparative and Applied Criminal Justice* 9(1):84-95.

Ebbie, O. (1989). "Crime and delinquency in metropolitan Lagos: A study of "crime and delinquency area theory." *Social Forces* 67(3):751-765.

Edwards, W. J. (1996). "Operating within the mainstream: Coping and adjustment among a sample of homosexual youths." *Deviant Behavior: An Interdisciplinary Journal* 17:229-251.

Edwards, W. J. (1996). A measurement of delinquency differences between a delinquent and non-delinquent sample: What are the implications? *Adolescence* 31(124):973-89.

Edwards, W. J. (1992). "Predicting juvenile delinquency: A review of correlates and a confirmation by recent research based on an integrated theoretical model." *Justice Quarterly* 9(4):553-84.

Edwards, W. J. (1992). "Constructing and testing a multiple-theory (integrated) model of juvenile delinquency." *Mid-American Review of Sociology* 17(1):31-43.

Fishman, L.T. (1994). "African American and Latino prisoners responses to a diagnosis of HIV/AIDS." In *African American Perspectives on Crime Causation, Criminal Justice Administration, and Crime Prevention.* Edited by A.T. Sulton. (Pp. 149-76). Englewood, CO: Sulton Books.

Fishman, L.T. (ed.). (1990). *Women at the wall: A study of prisoner's wives doing time on the outside.* Albany: State University of New York Press.

Georges-Abeyie, D. "Race, Ethnicity, and the Spatial Dynamic: Toward a Realistic Study of Black Crime, Crime Victimization, and Criminal Justice Processing of Blacks." *Social Justice* 16(4): 35-49.

Georges-Abeyie, D. (1983). "The Social Ecology of Bomb Threats, Dallas, Texas." *Journal of Black Studies* 13(3):305-20.

Georges, D. & Zandi, M. M. (1978). "The study of bombings, incendiaries, and bomb threats in the city of Dallas for the year 1975." *Journal of Environmental Systems* 8(1):57-97.

Greene, H. T. (1994). "Black perspectives on police brutality." In *African American Perspectives on Crime Causation, Criminal Justice Administration, and Crime Prevention.* Edited by A.T. Sulton. (Pp. 139-148). Englewood, CO: Sulton Books.

Greene, H. T. (1994) "Black female criminality." In *African American Perspectives on Crime Causation, Criminal Justice Administration, and Crime Prevention.* Edited by A.T. Sulton. (Pp. 109-122). Englewood, CO: Sulton Books.

Greene, H. T. (ed.). (1979). *A comprehensive bibliography of criminology and criminal justice literature by black authors from 1895 to 1978.* Hyattsville, MD: Ummah Publications.

Hawkins, D. F. (1995). "Ethnicity, race, and crime: A review of selected studies." In *Ethnicity, Race, and Crime: Perspectives Across Time and Place.* D.F. Hawkins (ed.), (Pp. 11-45). Albany: State University of New York Press.

Hawkins, D. F. (1993). "Inequality, culture, and interpersonal violence." *Interpersonal Violence* (Winter):80-94.

Hawkins, D. F. (1990). "Explaining the black homicide rate." *Journal of Interpersonal Violence* 5(2):151-163.

Hawkins, D. F. (1987). "Beyond anomalies: Rethinking the conflict perspective on race and criminal punishment." *Social Forces* 65(3):719-745.

Hawkins, D. F. (1986). "Race, crime type and imprisonment." *Justice Quarterly* 3(3):251-269.

Heard, C. A., Ludwig, W.G., & Bing, R.L. (1996). "Correlates of drug use among African American arrestees: The case for multi-cultural approaches." *The Journal of Research on Minority Affairs* 3:3-10.

Heard, C. A., & Bing, R.L. (eds.). (1995). *African American criminology and criminal justice directory.* Arlington: University of Texas at Arlington.

Heard, C. A. & Bing, R. L. (1993). "African American faculty and students on predominantly white university campuses." *Journal of Criminal Justice Education* 4(1):1-13.

Heard, C. A. (1993). "Forecasting models for managing a changing inmate population: Implications for public policy." *Criminal Justice Review* 18(1):1-11.

Henriques, Z. W. (1996). "Imprisoned mothers and their children: Separation-reunion syndrome dual impact." *Women and Criminal Justice* 8(1):77-95.

Henriques, Z. W. (1995). "African American women: The oppressive intersection of gender, race and class." *Women and Criminal Justice* 7(1):67-80.

Henriques, Z. W. (1981). "The human rights of incarcerated mothers and their children." *International Child Welfare Review* 49:18-27.

Huey, J. & Lynch, M. (1996). "The image of black women in criminology: Historical stereotypes as theoretical foundation." In *Justice with Prejudice: Race and Criminal Justice in America.* Edited by M.J. Lynch and E.B. Patterson. (pp. 72-88). New York: Harrow and Heston.

Jackson, J. E. & Ammen, S. (1996). "Race and correctional officers' punitive attitudes toward treatment programs for inmates." *Journal of Criminal Justice* 24(2):153-66.

Jackson, J. E. (1996). "Fraud masters: Professional credit card criminals and crime." *Criminal Justice Review* 19(1):24-55.

Jackson, J. E. (1996). "Computer crimes and criminals." *American Criminal Justice Association (LAE) Journal* 57(1/2):32-36.

Jackson, J. E., Wallace, P. H., & Wint, A.V. (1995). "The status of police officers' liability for negligence involving the use of firearms." *American Criminal Justice Association (LAE) Journal* 56 (Spring/Summer).

Jackson, J. E. (1993). "Fraud masters: Studying an illusory, non-violent, gang specializing in credit card crimes." *The Gang Journal* 1(4):17-36, 1993.

Jackson, J. E. (1992). "Deviance and change in the urban African American community." *Western Journal of Black Studies* 16(3):123-131.

Welsh, W., Harris, P., & **Jenkins, P.** (1996). "Reducing overrepresentation of minorities in juvenile justice: Development of community-based programs in Pennsylvania." *Crime and Delinquency* 42(1):76-98.

Jenkins, P. (1995). "School delinquency and school commitment." *Sociology of Education* 68(3):221-239.

Johnson, I. M. (1995). "Family members' perceptions of and attitudes toward elder abuse." *Families in Society* 76(4):220-229.

Curry, B.S., **Johnson, I. M.,** & Sigler, R.T. (1994). "Elder abuse: Justice problem, social problem, or research problem?" *Free Inquiry in Creative Sociology.* 22(1):65-71.

Johnson, I. M. (1992). "Economic, situational, and psychological correlates of the decision-making process of battered women." *Families in Society* 73(3):168-176.

Jones, D. & Brockett, R. (1995). "The role of the J.D. in criminal justice education." In *Issues in Criminal Justice: Shaping Tomorrow's Future*. N. Ali-Jackson (ed.). (Pp. 14-28). New York: McGraw-Hill.

Letman, S. T. & Spranza, F. G. (1978). "Some sociological perspectives on the immigration problem." *Journal of Humanics* 6(2):107-121.

Mann, C. R. (1995). "The contribution of institutionalized racism to minority crime." In *Ethnicity, Race and Crime*. Edited by D.F. Hawkins. Pp. 259-80. Albany: State University of New York Press.

Mann, C. R. (1994). "A Minority View of Juvenile Justice." *Washington and Lee Law Review,* 51(2):465-478.

Mann, C. R. (1995). "Seventeen white men and me." In *Individual Voices, Collective Visions: Fifty Years of Women in Sociology*. Edited by A. Goetting, & S. Fenstermaker. (Pp. 273-283). Philadelphia: Temple University Press.

Mann, C. R. (1990). "Female homicide and substance use: Is there a connection?" *Women and Criminal Justice* 1(2):87-109.

Mann, C. R. (1990). "Black female homicide in the United States." *Journal of Interpersonal Violence* 5(2):176-201.

Sheley, J.F., **McGee, Z. T.**, & Wright, J. (1995). "Weapon-Related Victimization in Selected Inner-City High Schools: A Final Summary Report Presented to the National Institute of Justice and the Office of Juvenile Justice and Delinquency Prevention. Washington, DC.

Sheley, J.F., **McGee, Z. T.**, & Wright, J. (1992). "Gun-related violence in and around inner-city schools." *American Journal of Diseases of Children* 146(June):677-682.

McGee, Z. T. (1992). "Social class differences in parental and peer influence on adolescent drug use." *Deviant Behavior: An Interdisciplinary Journal* 13:349-372.

McMurray, H. L. (1993). "High risk parolees in transition from institution to community life." *Journal of Offender Rehabilitation* 19:145-161.

Leashore, B.R., **McMurray, H. L.** & Bailey, B. C. (1992). "Reuniting and preserving African American families." In *Child Welfare: An Afrocentric perspective.* Joyce E. Everett, Sandra S. Chipungu, and Bogart R. Leashore, (eds.). (Pp. 247-265). New Brunswick, NJ: Rutgers University Press.

McMurray, H. L. (1990). "Attitudes of assaulted police officers and their policy implications." *Journal of Police Science and Administration* 17:44-48.

Okereke, Godpower O. (1993). "Public attitudes toward the police force in Nigeria." *Police Studies* 16(3):113-121.

Oli, S. I. (1994). "A dichotomization: Crime and criminality among traditional and Christianized Igbo." In *African American Perspectives on Crime Causation, Criminal Justice Administration, and Crime Prevention.* Edited by Ann T. Sulton. (Pp. 17-32). Englewood, CO: Sulton Books.

Oliver, W. (1989). "Sexual conquest and patterns of black-on-black violence: A structural-cultural perspective." *Violence and Victims* 4(4):257-273.

Oliver, W. (1989). "Black males and social problems: Prevention through Afrocentric socialization." *Journal of Black Studies* 20(1):15-39.

Pettiway, L. (1995). "Copping crack: The travel behavior of crack users." *Justice Quarterly* 12(3):499-524.

Pettiway, L. (1988). "Urban spatial structure and incidence of arson: Differences between ghetto and nonghetto environments." *Justice Quarterly* 5(1):113-29.

Pettiway, L. (1987). "Participation in crime partnerships by female drug users: The effects of domestic arrangements, drug use, and criminal involvement." *Criminology* 25(3):741-66.

Pettiway, L. (1987)."Arson for revenge: The role of environmental situation, age, sex and race." *Journal of Quantitative Criminology* 3(2):169-184.

Quimby, E. (1995). "Homeless clients' perspectives on recovery in the Washington, DC, dual diagnosis project." *Contemporary Drug Problems* 22(2):265-289.

Quimby, E. (1993). "Obstacles to reducing AIDS among African Americans." *Journal of Black Psychology* 19(2):215-222.

Quimby, E. (1990). "Drug trafficking and the Caribbean connection: Survival mechanisms, entrepreneurship and social symptoms." *Urban League Review* 14(2):61-70.

Ross, L. E. (1996). "The relationship between religion, self-esteem, and delinquency." *Journal of Crime and Justice* 19(2):195-214.

Ross, L. E. (1995). "School environment, self-esteem, and delinquency." *Journal of Criminal Justice* 23(6):555-567.

Ross, L. E. (1994). "The impact of race-esteem and self-esteem on delinquency." *Sociological Focus* 27(2):111-129.

Ross, L. E. (1994). "Religion and deviance: Exploring the impact of social control elements." *Sociological Spectrum* (14):65-86.

Ross, L. E. (1992). "Blacks, self-esteem, and delinquency: It's time for a new approach." *Justice Quarterly* 9(4):609-624.

Russell, K. (1996). "The racial hoax as crime: The law as affirmation." *Indiana Law Journal* 71(3):594-621.

Russell, K. (1994). "A critical view from the inside: An application of critical legal studies to criminal law and criminology." *Journal of Criminal Law and Criminology* 85(1):222-40.

Russell, K. (1994). "The racial inequality hypothesis: A critical look at the research and an alternative theoretical analysis." *Law and Human Behavior* 18(3):305-17.

Russell, K. (1994). "The constitutionality of jury override in Alabama death penalty cases." *Alabama Law Review* 46(1):5-45.

Russell, K. (1992). "Development of a black criminology and the role of the black criminologist." *Justice Quarterly* 9(4):667-84.

Scott. E. (1994). "Reducing the involvement of African American males in the criminal justice system." In *African American Perspectives on Crime Causation, Criminal Justice Administration, and Crime Prevention.* Edited by Ann T. Sulton, (Pp. 185-200). Englewood, CO: Sulton Books.

Scott, E. (1975). "Black attitudes toward crime and crime prevention." In *Crime and Its Impact on the Black Community.* Edited by L.E. Gary and L.P. Brown. (pp. 13-30). Washington, DC: Howard University Institute for Urban Affairs and Research.

Johnson, J. B. & **P.E. Secret.** (1995). "The effects of court structure on juvenile court decisionmaking." *Journal of Criminal Justice* 23(1):63-82.

Secret, P. E. & Johnson, J.B. (1989). "Racial difference in attitudes toward crime control." *Journal of Criminal Justice* 17:361-375.

Stokes, L. D. & Scott, J.F. (1996). "Affirmative action and selected minority groups in law enforcement." *Journal of Criminal Justice* 24(1):29-38.

Stokes, L. D. & Venters, K. (1993). "Black homicide in a midsize southern city, 1980-1989." *American Journal of Criminal Justice* 17(2):61-71.

Sulton, A.T. (1994). "Preventing crime through economic development in urban neighborhoods." In *African American Perspectives on Crime Causation, Criminal Justice Administration, and Crime Prevention.* Edited by A.T. Sulton. (pp. 201-22). Englewood, CO: Sulton Books.

Sulton, A.T. (ed.). (1994). *African American Perspectives on Crime Causation, Criminal Justice Administration, and Crime Prevention.* Englewood, CO: Sulton Books.

Tatum, B. L. (1996). "An analysis of factors contributing to the delinquency of the black youth." *Journal of Black Studies* 26(3):356-368.

Tatum, B. L. (1994). "The colonial model as a theoretical explanation of crime and delinquency." In *African American Perspectives on Crime Causation, Criminal Justice Administration and Crime Prevention.* Edited by A.T. Sulton. (Pp. 33-52). Englewood, CO: Sulton Books.

Taylor, D. L. & Bing, R.L. (1995). "Racial discrimination in the juvenile justice system: Some unanswered questions." *Challenge* 6(2):5-28.

Taylor, D. L. (1994) "Family and Delinquency: African American Female Headed Households and Chronic Maladaptive Behavior of Juveniles." In *African American Perspectives on Crime Causation, Criminal Justice Administration, and Crime Prevention.* Edited by Ann T. Sulton. (pp. 124-38). Englewood, CO: Sulton Books.

Taylor, D. L., Chitwood, D.D., McElrath, K., and Belgrave, L.L. (1994). "Ethnicity, social support, and injection drug use." *Journal of Black Psychology* 20(1):36-46.

Whitson, M. & Moyer, I. (1994) "Patriarchy, power differentials, and women offenders." In I.L. Moyer (Ed.), *The Changing Role of Women in the Criminal Justice System*, 2nd Edition. (pp. 31-56). Prospect Heights, IL: Waveland Press.

Williams, J. J. (1995). "Type of counsel and the outcome of criminal appeals: A research note." *American Journal of Criminal Justice* 19(2).

Williams, J. J. (1995). "Race of appellant, sentencing guidelines, and decisionmaking in criminal appeals: A research note." *Journal of Criminal Justice* 23(1):83-91.

Williams, J. J. (1994). "Controlling the Judge's Discretion: Appellate Review of Departures Made in Sentencing Guideline Cases." *The Justice System Journal* 17(2):229-240.

Williams, J. J. (1992). "Sentencing guidelines and the changing composition of criminal appeals: A preliminary analysis." *Judicature* 76(2):94-96.

Williams, J. J. (1991). "Predicting Decisions Rendered in Criminal Appeals." *Journal of Criminal Justice* 19:463-469.

Wilson, G. P. & McMurray, H. L. (1990). *Durham County Jail Population Management Plan.* Durham, NC: UNC-Central Department of Criminal Justice.

Wilson, G. P., Cullen, F. T., Latessa, E. J. & Wills, J.S. (1985). "State Intervention and Victimless Crimes: A Study of Police Attitudes" *Journal of Police Science and Administration*, 13(1):22-29.

Wilson, G. P. (1983). "Halfway House Programs for Offenders." *Probation, Parole, and Community Corrections: A Reader.* Edited by Lawrence F. Travis III. (Pp. 151-164). Prospect Heights, IL: Waveland Press.

Wright, B. S. & Senese, J.D. (1996). "An analysis of selected aspects of police training." *Journal of Contemporary Criminal Justice* 12(3):235-49.

Wright, B. S. (1993) "An examination of gender issues that were observed in the proportion of arrests over time." In *Female Criminality: The State of the Art.* Edited by C.C. Culliver. (Pp. 305-20). New York: Garland Publishing.

Wright, B. S., Doerner, W.G., & Speir, J.C. (1990). "Pre-employment psychological testing as a predictor of police performance during an FTO program." *American Journal of Police* 9(4):65-83.

Doerner, W.G., Spier, J.C., & **Wright, B. S.** (1989). "An analysis of rater-ratee race and sex influences upon field training officer program evaluations." *Journal of Criminal Justice* 17(2):103-114.

Young, V. & Greene, H.T. (1995). "Pedagogical Reconstruction: Incorporating African American Perspectives into the Curriculum." *Journal of Criminal Justice Education.* 6(1):85-104.

Young, V. (1994). "The politics of disproportionality." In *African American Perspectives on Crime Causation, Criminal Justice Administration, and Crime Prevention.* Edited by Ann T. Sulton. (Pp. 69-81). Englewood, CO: Sulton Books.

Young, V. & Sulton, A.T. (1991). "Excluded: The current status of African American scholars in the field of criminology and criminal justice." *Journal of Research in Crime and Delinquency.* 28:101-16.

Appendix: Doctoral Dissertations of African American Criminologists (1970–1996)

Agozino, Biko. (1993). *Black women and the criminal justice system.* University of Edinburgh. Ph.D. in Criminology.

Austin, Roy L. (1973). *Interpersonal maturity level theory and evaluation.* University of Washington. Ph.D. in Sociology.

Bailey, Frankie (1986). *Boundary maintenance, interest-group conflict, and Black justice in Danville, Virginia, 1900-1930.* State University of New York at Albany. Ph.D. in Criminology.

Bing, Robert L., III (1988). *Plea bargaining: An analysis of the empirical evidence.* Florida State University-Tallahassee. Ph.D. in Criminology.

Brown, Lee P. (1968). *Evaluation of a police-community relations program.* University of California-Berkeley. Ph.D. in Criminology.

Browning, Sandra L. (1997). *A marriage wasteland: Marital misperceptions of black women.* University of Cincinnati. Ph.D. in Sociology.

Corley, Charles J. (1986). *Socio-economic and attitudinal correlates of marital instability: A longitudinal assessment.* Bowling Green State University. Ph.D. in Sociology.

Coston, Charisse T. (1988). *An explanation of the fear of crime among shopping-bag ladies in New York City.* Rutgers State University. Ph.D. in Criminology

Debro, Julius (1975). *Institutional racism in federal sentencing.* University of California-Berkeley. Ph.D. in Criminology.

Dorsey, R. Rita (1993). *Higher education for police officers: An analysis of the relationship between higher education, police systems, and cultural awareness.* University of Mississippi. Ph.D. in Higher Education with cognates in Criminal Justice.

Ebbie, Obi. (1981). *Crime in Nigeria: An analysis of characteristics of offenders incarcerated in Nigerian prisons.* Southern Illinois University-Carbondale. Ph.D. in Criminology.

Edwards, Willie J. (1989). *Juvenile delinquent involvement, a multivariate explanation: An integration of several sociological theories into a single causal model.* University of Minnesota. Ph.D. in Criminology.

Fishman, Laura T. (1983). *Women at the wall: A study of prisoners' wives doing time on the outside.* McGill University (Canada). Ph.D. in Sociology.

Georges-Abeyie, Daniel E. (1974). *Arson: The ecology of urban unrest in an American city--Newark, New Jersey, a case study of collective violence.* Syracuse University. Ph.D. in Criminology.

Gilbert, Evelyn (1990). *The social ecology of elderly homicide.* Florida State University-Tallahassee. Ph.D. in Criminology.

Greene, Helen T. (1988). *The effects of police systems and their environments on police homicides: An exploratory analysis.* University of Maryland-College Park. Ph.D. in Criminology.

Hawkins, Darnell F. (1976). *Nonresponse in Detroit area study*

surveys: A ten-year analysis. University of Michigan. Ph.D. in Sociology. Juris Doctor, 1981.

Heard, Chinita A. (1988). *Factors influencing the decision-making process in the substantiation of child sexual abuse cases*. Florida State University-Tallahassee. Ph.D. in Criminology.

Henriques, Zelma W. (1979). *Incarcerated mothers' perceptions of their children's situation: A descriptive and analytical study*. Columbia University Teachers College. Ed.D. in Applied Human Development and Counseling Psychology.

Huey, Jacqueline F. (1994). *Historical analysis of the development of a feminist-oriented criminology*. Florida State University-Tallahassee. Ph.D. in Criminology.

Jackson, Jerome E. (1992). *The impact of less punitive values upon the role perceptions of correctional officers and their attitudes toward treatment programs for inmates in the Texas Department of Criminal Justice-Institutional Division*. Sam Houston State University-Huntsville. Ph.D. in Criminology.

Jenkins, Patricia H. (1993) *School delinquency and the school social bond*. University of Delaware-Newark. Ph.D. in Sociology. Juris Doctor, 1991.

Johnson, Ida M. (1987). *Wife abuse: Factors predictive of the decision-making process of battered women*. Florida State University-Tallahassee. Ph.D. in Criminology.

Jones-Brown, Delores L. (1996). *Race and legal socialization*. Rutgers University. Ph.D. in Criminology. Juris Doctor, 1985.

Letman, Sloan, DePaul University. Juris Doctor, 1975.

Mann, Coramae R. (1976). *The juvenile female in the judicial process*. University of Illinois at Chicago Circle. Ph.D. in

Sociology.

McGee, Zina T. (1994). *Criminal victimization among inner-city high school students.* Tulane University. Ph.D. in Sociology.

McMurray, Harvey L. (1988). *Police post-assault reactions and the buffering effects of social support.* Rutgers University. Ph.D. in Criminology.

Okereke, Godpower O. (1992). *The social organization of Nigerian law enforcement: Its effects on police-public relations.* Oklahoma State University-Stillwater. Ph.D. in Sociology.

Oli, Sampson I. (1984). *Crime and social control in Nigeria: Growth of a quandary.* City University of New York. Ph.D. in Criminology.

Oliver, William (1993). *Violent confrontations between black males in bars and bar settings.* State University of New York at Albany. Ph.D. in Criminology.

Pettiway, Leon E. (1979). *A geographical description of robbery and burglary offense locations in Milwaukee County.* University of Wisconsin-Milwaukee. Ph.D. in Urban Geography.

Quimby, Ernest (1977). *Black political development in Bedford-Stuyvesant Restoration Corporation.* City University of New York. Ph.D. in Sociology.

Ross, Lee E. (1991). *Christian religiosity and deviance re-examined: An application and extension of social control theory.* Rutgers University. Ph.D. in Criminology.

Russell, Katheryn K. (1992). *Trial by jury, death by judge: An empirical and legal analysis of jury override in Alabama.* University of Maryland-College Park. Ph.D. in Criminology. Juris Doctor, 1986.

Scott, Elsie L. (1980). *The politics of the police system in predominantly black cities.* Atlanta University. Ph.D. in Criminology.

Secret, Philip E. (1978). *Racial differences in political participation and attitudes toward protest.* University of Nebraska-Lincoln. Ph.D. in Political Science.

Stokes, Larry D. (1990). *Policy intervention in social problems development: A case for affirmative action.* Howard University. Ph.D. in Sociology.

Sulton, Ann T. (1984). *Prediction of individuals participation to mechanical crime prevention activities.* University of Maryland. Ph.D. in Criminology.

Tatum, Becky L. (1996). *Race, class, alienation and delinquency: Assessing motivational factors through the application of structural models.* State University of New York, Albany. Ph.D. in Criminology.

Taylor, Dorothy L. (1989). *An assessment of factors related to female-headed households and their effect upon juvenile chronic maladaptive behavior in African American families.* Florida State University-Tallahassee. Ph.D. in Criminology.

Whitson, Marian H. (1995). *Crime and social control: Perceptions of religiously active black women of the Christian Methodist Episcopal Church.* Indiana University. Ph.D. in Criminology. Juris Doctor, 1984.

Williams, Jimmy J. (1989). *Courts and politics: A quantitative analysis of lawyers and criminal appeal cases.* Florida State University. Ph.D. in Criminology.

Wilson, George P. (1983). *An analysis of the relationship between MMPI and demographic factors for escapees in minimum* *security environment.* Michigan State University. Ph.D. in Criminology.

Wright, Benjamin S. (1988). *Psychological evaluations as predictors of police recruit performance.* Florida State University. Ph.D. in Criminology.

Young, Vernetta D. (1981). *Patterns of female criminality.* State University of New York at Albany. Ph.D. in Criminology.

Author and Subject Index

About the Author

LEE E. ROSS is associate professor of Criminal Justice in the School of Social Welfare at the University of Wisconsin-Milwaukee, where he teaches courses on victimology, domestic violence, research methods, and race, crime, and justice. He has written extensively on the relationship between religion, self-esteem, and delinquency, and his most recent work examines the publication experiences of African American criminologists.

ISBN 0-313-30150-6

90000>

9 780313 301506

HARDCOVER BAR CODE

EAN